HE
LEADS
ME

Adventures in God

Workbook

A Happy Walk Book

RENNIE DU PLESSIS
A VICTOR

Cover Design Ligeia Vagharshagian
Cover image CC0
https://pixabay.com/vectors/smiley-happy-smile-face-abstract-1293338/

Disclaimer
This book is not intended to provide medical advice or to take the place of medical advice and treatment from your personal physician. Readers must consult a qualified health professional regarding the treatment of any medical problems. The authors do not take any responsibility for any possible consequences from any action or application to any person reading or following the information in this book.

Website information is correct at the time of publishing. However, no liability can be accepted for any information or links found on third-party websites which are subject to change.

Unless otherwise indicated, Bible quotations are quoted or adapted from the New King James version of the Bible.

FREE BOOK OFFER

Create more success and fulfilment in your life. Discover more about yourself, your God-given destiny, and develop it. Use an easy, effective system designed by an expert in Christian living and positive psychology. It's life changing.

Get your copy here
https://www.subscribepage.com/faith-based-living

CONTENTS

WHICH WAY NOW?

You hold me by my right hand. You will guide me with Your counsel, and afterward receive me to glory." Psalm 73:23-24

Excerpt from 'Make your Prayers Work: A Happy Walk Book'
https://www.amazon.co.uk/dp/B0B22YL7RX

This so beautifully shows God's leading and the verse reveals just how powerful and eternal that leading is. Asaph, the writer of Psalm 73 recounts some of the things he faced and the path he decided to take in life: **he took God's hand.** In that action is the peace he, just like we, find: the guidance in life through counsel and glory at the end of our earthly journey. **Think about that for a moment. In all situations, God is holding your hand, guiding you with perfect counsel for the rest of your life!**

Asaph understood the key to living in continuous guidance, and started this verse off by stating that truth: "Nevertheless I am continually with You." It was because Asaph stayed in contact with and connected to God that he could say with assurance "You hold me by my right hand," and he knew the guidance that comes through God's counsel.

Living in a world that is always 'on' where noise and busyness is all around and you are constantly pinged can become all that your life is. There is a solution to this distraction - simply take time where you decide in the midst of all this that your priority is to stay connected to God, and you will expand your life. In the presence of God is all fullness, all power, all possibility – just connect. Take His hand. It's a gesture of intimacy, up close and personal, where God walks beside you. It's also a gesture of willingness on your part to be led by God.

This is the loving God you are connected to, the God you love and who loves you. He wants to talk to you, walk with you, show you His wisdom and share in the joy of your wonderful life unfolding. He's going to speak to you and wants you to speak to Him as you walk side by side.

Connecting = leading.

Having this connection doesn't mean you have to be listening in prayer every moment of the day. You don't have to lock yourself away in solitary confinement. You don't have to become a wilderness dwelling hermit. You can still enjoy life and living and all your social interactions. **What it does mean is that you purpose in your heart to make it a priority to connect with God every day and to not let go of His hand.** The best way to do that is in a quiet time of prayer.

"Call to Me, and I will answer you, and show you great and mighty things, which you do not know." Jeremiah 33:3. The God of all the universe issues an invitation to you: "Call to Me." God wants a personal connection with you and wants to have communication with you. Think about that, the Creator of all things wants you to reach out to Him, talk to Him and relate with Him.

He follows it up with a promise: "and I will answer you." Not I might, or perhaps, but a definite "I will." That means He's listening for your call, He's involved in your life and excited to "show you great and mighty things, which you do not know." When you call God answers by showing you great and mighty things. **He is going to lead you and give you amazing things that will make your life an adventure in God.**

In holding God's hand, you know you can only go where He goes, He's leading. And by your decision and action to spend time in prayer every day you create the powerful habit that will sensitize your heart to hearing and responding to God's leading. You'll get to understand where God is leading you.

Connecting = empowered living.

Why is it that of all the things the disciples could've asked of Jesus to teach them their only recorded request is: "Lord teach us how to pray"?

They could've asked how to perform miracles, heal, but they asked for teaching on prayer. Why would they ask Jesus for this? After all, the disciples were Jewish men taught how to pray at a young age. So, why the request? Because in Jesus they saw a new dimension to prayer, full of power. They didn't ask to learn how to perform miracles because they knew that everything Jesus did stemmed from His prayer and communion. They realized in order to do what He did consistently they needed to copy Him in His prayer life.

Prayer is the starting point.

Prayer is talking to and listening to God and God intended that you use your prayer to get to know Him and access all the kingdom power available to you. God will lead deeper into this kingdom knowledge and that will open and expand your abilities to use prayer the way God intended: **as an effective tool to speak to God and create through prayer and to be led to blessings in your life.**

Many years ago, my partner was on an overseas assignment. While in prayer I had a very clear message for him and when he phoned me, I shared it. 'Someone you know in ministry has a job for you.' Now, he wasn't looking for other work at that time. Still, he took what the Spirit revealed to heart and prayerfully pondered over what was revealed. Then, he had a very strong sense, upon reflection on this, to contact a specific person in the television industry. The man was amazed as he had a newly created position not yet advertised. My partner was offered this lucrative job on the spot. A few years later, this same man opened another door for us when we came to England that smoothed out a difficult move from overseas. Through this we were able, with the leading of God, to build a wonderful, enlarged life filled with blessing, peace and abundance.

We weren't looking for a blessing. My partner already had a job but God led him to a better, more lucrative one. Our extravagant God didn't stop there – the blessing that came through my partner being obedient to God's leading to contact this person led to knock on effects into other parts of our life. And it all started while I was in prayer.

Spending time with God opens you up to hear God and understand His leading. Prayer strengthens your connection and empowers you for living and opens you to all the amazing ways God will lead you. Mentally, when your focus is in one place as it is when you pray, you are able to 'see' that place of focus more clearly and fully. Because your attention is on the kingdom you are more aware of what's going on there and what you should do in your life.

An added dimension to the leading of God.

"Then your light shall break forth like the morning, your healing shall spring forth speedily, and your righteousness shall go before you; The glory of the Lord shall be your rear guard." Isaiah 58:8. This is only part of the promises of combining fasting with praying. God showed me that fasting and praying are like the two wings of an eagle, you need both "to mount up on wings of eagles".

5

Fasting has many, many benefits, if done correctly, and if you'd like to know more about fasting, the empowerment that comes through it, the health benefits and how to do it the right way, we recommend 'Make your Prayers Work: A Happy Walk Book.'

https://www.amazon.co.uk/dp/B0B22YL7RX

Here, we're focusing on the benefits to being led by God through fasting and prayer. "Then you shall call, and the Lord will answer; You shall cry, and He will say, 'Here I am.' Then your light shall dawn in the darkness, and your darkness shall be as the noonday. The Lord will guide you continually..." See Isaiah 58:9 & 11.

You'll call to God and he'll say, "I'm here." He's listening to help you. And he'll keep guiding you in life.

That's a staggering promise. Fasting done correctly brings you into closer communion with God. In other words, fasting enhances your personal prayer time. It maximises your ability to speak to God, have His response and receive His guidance in your life. And, as a result it must bring us a more orderly, successful life, health and abundance in all forms. And it affects our ability to help others through our prayers and the leading of God.

In this book, we will explore some of the ways God leads and how you can become more sensitive to that leading by recognising God's voice in different situations. There are many ways that God leads, some subtle, some clear. Being able to recognize the leading God does in your life, no matter what method He uses, will open untold blessings to you.

Prayer: "I'm taking Your hand so You can walk beside me and lead me. I will come to You every day to speak with You and listen to You and be with You because I love you. Lead me today in all I do."

Come with us as we look through the bible to see how God led others and what that teaches us about His leading. And discover how you can incorporate it into your life for greater blessing. My partner and I will share some real life adventures that we and others experienced through the leading of God and the wonderful results that happened.

This is my time

Here's a checklist of key points to help you see God's leading in your life and any steps you need to take.

-I make the decision to take God's hand so that God walks beside me and leads me.

-I will come to God every day to speak with Him.

-I will listen to Him to receive His counsel.

-I choose to let God lead me every day in all I do.

-I am expectant that God will show me amazing things

because I choose to stay connected to Him.

-I am expectant that God will release power into my life because I choose to stay connected to Him.

-I understand that I benefit in many ways by fasting including having clearer leading, And I have studied how to fast correctly and safely.

-I choose to fast with prayer and listening regularly.

How did you go?

Did you find that you're doing everything in the checklist?

Yes? Congratulations! Your foundation to be led by God every day is in place.

No? No problem! You now know what steps to take to activate greater leading in your life.

Steps I will take

-On a sheet of paper or in a journal set down any steps you need to make or any of the keys you want to keep an eye on. (To know more about fasting and doing it the right: 'Make your Prayers Work.' https://www.amazon.co.uk/dp/B0B22YL7RX)

Coming up

God leads us as our good Shepherd. What does that really mean in our life and what can we expect? Let's find out ...

WHOLENESS IN LIFE

"The Lord is my Shepherd; I shall not want. He makes me to lie down in green pastures; He leads me beside the still waters." Psalm 23:1-2.

Imagine you've stepped into a serene and peaceful picture. Everything is still and calm, not a ripple on the water. You feel peaceful and at rest, filled with joy at the wonder of being surrounded by so much beauty. It's that place of perfect wholeness you find only in the stillness of nature. You're content and at peace.

Can we find this in real life? Yes! Psalm 23 paints the picture of the faithful Shepherd, ever guarding and guiding to the safest and best pastures for us to find rest and refreshment. David is writing from experience, remembering when he cared for his father's flocks and the care he took with that flock – to the point of risking his life to rescue a lamb.

What will we find after being led to still waters?

God provides for His people, not only food and rest, but refreshment also and pleasure. Having the Lord as your Shepherd you are assured of being led to still waters – that place in the midst of green pastures where there's no lack. The assurance of our Shepherd leading and guiding follows us through the bible and Jesus picks up that theme, declaring Himself the good Shepherd. John 10:11. We are led into His fold, a place of safety and abundance, we hear His voice and follow, secure under His protection.

Being led to still waters and green pastures is much more than a place of peace and abundance. It's through God's leading that we find restoration and wholeness. "He restores my soul; He leads me in the paths of righteousness for His name's sake." Psalm 23:3. By following that right path, everything falls into place. When life just crowds out your peace and centredness in God, He will lead you to restoration. In heartache and pain, He leads to restoration – a point beyond where you are, where you are healed of the hurt and restored to newness of life.

It doesn't mean everything will always be perfect. You will know hardships and troubles in life, everyone does. But in those dark times or times of uncertainty, our Shepherd is there. "Even if I walk through the valley of the shadow of death" it holds no fear for believers because there's no substantial evil in it.

Just like the shadow of a snake cannot sting, it's just a shadow, death is just a graduation to glory. And we are walking through that valley, led by God, we're not camping there. We are being led onward in abundance and toward glory! Our comfort is in the fact that nothing, not even death can separate us from the love of God.

"I will fear no evil; for You are with me; Your rod and Your staff, they comfort me." We live in the world in the security that nothing can touch us unless we let it. Our loving God is with us, through His Word, His Spirit, signs, wonders, miracles and 'thin places'. We simply have to connect, listen and respond to every form of God's leading we encounter in our days to access all His comfort and abundance. Plentiful provision is made for our bodies, for our souls, for our life now and for the life that's to come.

"You prepare a table before me in the presence of my enemies" means you sit down to a feast in total safety and peace while your enemies look on. No matter what situation you face, there is peace at the table of God. Find sustenance in God's word, enjoy the bread of life, be watered by the Spirit, then turn your attention to the abundance you have in this life now and enjoy it.

"You anoint my head with oil; My cup runs over." Anointing has to do with empowering by the Spirit. And your cup running over indicates abundance.

"Surely goodness and mercy shall follow me all the days of my life; and I will dwell in the house of the Lord forever." Surely means it's a sure thing. Psalm 23 ends with the assurance of a life filled with goodness and mercy in all its forms.

We have a fountain of mercy, pardoning mercy, protecting mercy, sustaining mercy, supplying mercy.

This is life long - the goodness and mercy cannot be used up and is new every morning. Lamentations 3:23.

Goodness and mercy having followed you all the days of your life on this earth, when that is ended, you are led to "dwell in the house of the Lord for ever."

Every aspect and facet of wholeness is offered in the wholeness of being led by God. Psalm 23 is the picture of wholeness, rest, health, refreshment, abundance and empowered living. And it's yours to live as you walk beside a God who leads you constantly and carefully into all good things – in this life and the life to come.

Prayer: "Thank you Shepherd of my life, for Your daily leading. Help me to be sensitive to every opportunity You will lead me into today so I can access every good thing for my life and the lives of those around me."

This is my time

God is your shepherd – what an amazing way to describe being led. In Psalm 23 and John 10:11 we looked at the fullness of what it means to have God as our caring shepherd who leads, guides, and protects us.

Check through the key points below and note all those things you can see that God's already doing and identify any that are missing at present. Let's go:

-Wholeness, abundance, peace, safety, rest, refreshment, restoration, health, empowered living, contentment, pleasure, leading into the best you can be as a person, mercy, forgiveness, expectancy that you have life with God forever.

How did you go?

It's encouraging to note all the ways God blesses us as He leads us as our good Shepherd.

Did you find anything missing at present? Sometimes, we go through temporary difficulty like upright Job. He said, "... when God has tested me, I will emerge as pure gold." Job 23:10. God gave him far more afterwards. David who wrote about God as his shepherd experienced many of life's challenges (and some were of his own making). He knew God would lead him through all of them as his shepherd. So, be encouraged - our God is leading you right now to green pastures, still waters and a pleasant life - goodness and mercy actively pursue you all the days of your life.

Remember that our loving God is with us, through His Word, His Spirit, signs, wonders, miracles and 'thin places'. We simply have to connect, listen and respond to every form of God's leading to access all His comfort and abundance.

We can trust that God will lead us constantly and carefully into all good things.

Steps I will take

-Celebrate with gratitude. Whether everything's perfect in your life right now or not, thank God for all you see He's done and does for you.

-Stay connected, listen and respond to anything God leads you to do.

-If there's anything missing in your life, ask God to show you if you're doing everything right. Whatever He shows you that needs change, be ready to change.

-Stay expectant like Job and David because God is truly leading you as your shepherd to bless your life and make you a blessing.

Coming up

Knowing what the leading of God gives us in abundant living, let's explore how God leads...

HOW DOES GOD LEAD?

"...send out Your light and Your truth! Let them lead me." Psalm 43:3.

Three hundred men stood looking down at the hundreds of lights and campfires below them. The Midianite camp swarmed with a people secure and careless in their strength as the camp prepared for the night.

The three hundred watched quietly, hardly moving – a small band of men on a mission waiting for the right moment. How did so few dare to come against the might of Midian? The Lord led them to this moment in time so that the victory of Israel's deliverance would be His. This is how it happened:

After seven long years under the oppression of the Midianites, Israel rose up and thirty two thousand men able to do battle gathered to Gideon. Judges 7. God led Gideon to announce, "Whoever is fearful and afraid, let him turn and depart at once from Mount Gilead." Two thirds turned back and ten thousand remained.

God wanted a mighty, impossible victory for Israel and tells Gideon to lead the men to water and watch their behaviour as they drank. God commands,

"Everyone who laps from the water with his tongue, as a dog laps, you shall set apart by himself; likewise everyone who gets down on his knees to drink." So, two groups.

By far the larger group of men were those who got down on their knees, over nine thousand men. They were vulnerable to attack because they lacked vigilance. In contrast, those who lapped the water out of a cupped hand can spring into action at anything they see. And it is with this group of merely three hundred men that God promises, "By the three hundred men who lapped I will save you, and deliver the Midianites into your hand."

Gideon has his mighty men, handpicked by God's leading. "Then he divided the three hundred men into three companies, and he put a trumpet into every man's hand, with empty pitchers, and torches inside the pitchers." In the middle watch Gideon and his men moved to the edge of the camp and spread out around the edge of the camp with this instruction: "When I blow the trumpet, I and all who are with me, then you also blow the trumpets on every side of the whole camp, and say, 'The sword of the Lord and of Gideon!'"

As the sound and light from the three hundred pierced the darkness around the Midianite camp, chaos broke out amongst the Midianites and "the whole army ran and cried out and fled. The Lord set every man's sword against his companion throughout the whole camp; and the army fled." Gideon sends out a call to all Israel to come together and share in the victory with him and his mighty men as he rids Israel of Midian oppression.

Lessons in leading from Gideon.

Gideon was not a leader when God led him in this mighty deliverance and throughout Judges 6 & 7, we see Gideon grow in his trust and reliance on God through his encounters with the Angel of the Lord. He learns to follow the instructions given him and those actions force him out of his comfort zone and it grows him as a leader.

God's objective in His encounter with Gideon was to deliver Israel out of the hand of the Midianites. God always has an objective to His leading. Whether it's that daily leading of God that ensures you are safe, abundant, growing or experiencing more of God, or something huge, there is always an objective. **If you understand God's objective, it's easier to flow in His leading.**

The best way to find out what God's objective is: Take time to listen and pray in quiet time with God. Gideon offered sacrifices to God, a way to bring his focus back to God. We no longer need to do that to connect to God because Jesus was the ultimate, once-and-for-always sacrifice. Our quiet time with God will reveal what's on God's heart. And God will lead in other ways too.

God will lead your through...

- **Prayer and fasting** - There are many different types of prayer you can use to strengthen your sensitivity to God's leading. One such way is praying in tongues. When praying in your personal tongue, you speak mysteries with God and these mysteries is God depositing into your heart concerning your future and how He's leading you. To understand the different unknown tongues and how to operate in them we recommend 'The Holy Spirit Book.'
  https://www.amazon.co.uk/dp/B086N4PRBT

- **The Holy Spirit** - He is your Counsellor, Guide and Comforter because you are a child of God. Romans 8:14. This leading can take the form of a prompting in your heart, a message or a still small voice speaking to your spirit as you seek God's will. Acts 13:2. 'The Holy Spirit Book' covers this in depth.

- **The bible** - This is your manual for life and contains all that you need to grow as a person and grow in your relationship with God and others. Spend time in your bible. Don't just read it once and move on, study it until it becomes as natural as breathing and you understand and can apply what your read. "Your word is a lamp to my feet and a light to my path." Psalm 119:105.

- **Gifts of the Spirit like prophecy, word of knowledge and word of wisdom** - All three of these Gifts work as the Spirit wills and has God's objective behind it. With all three of these Gifts

18

you need mature, bible-based believers to assess and assist you in the leading you are getting through the Gift. 1 Corinthians 12 & 14. To know more about these and the other Gifts and their operations, we recommend 'The Holy Spirit Book.' https://www.amazon.co.uk/dp/B086N4PRBT

- **Dreams** - God may use a dream to confirm His objective in your life or to prepare you for a paradigm shift in your life. There are different types of dreams: dreams used by our minds to process our day, spirit dreams that are vivid and have some spiritual significance and lucid dreams where you dream while in an alert and aware state and you can control that dream. Understanding the difference will help you know which dreams are a part of God leading and what you should do about the dream.

- **Visions** - As visions can be induced through various methods, it's important to make sure that what you're seeing is from God. There are open visions where you are in two places at once, both in the present and in the vision. There are visions where you are physically transported to another place Ezekiel 8:3, or you see into the spirit realm. Each type of vision serves a different purpose.

- **'Thin places'** - These are special physical places where all of God's presence and eternal heaven breaks through for a very specific reason. If you want to know more about thin places, we recommend 'God's 'Thin Places' https://www.amazon.co.uk/dp/B09XLLCFVL

- **Mature, bible-based believers and leaders sensitive to the voice of God** - God may give you a thought, an impression, or a deepening sense of conviction or clarity. But it's easy to confuse our own desires with God's will. Any kind of leading you think is from God must line up squarely with the bible, should be in line with other things God has already revealed to you, should not be harmful to others, should fulfil God's objective and should also be confirmed by mature believers (especially if it involves something you are emotional about or desire very strongly). "Plans go wrong for lack of advice; many advisers bring success." Proverbs 15:22 NLT Don't make decisions without getting advice. Make sure you talk to the right people, those who love God and understand His word. Don't just ask in order to confirm what you want to hear. Listen to what your advisors say. Proverbs 11:14.

God's leading means two things: we're being led home to God in heaven and so we're purifying and preparing ourselves each day for the sight of Christ. That is where our compass is pointing every single day. That is the general direction, but then there is something more. God will reveal the next immediate stage to us, a few more steps, day by day so we can grow in trust and maturity, and to bless and increase us.

Each one of us believers, regardless of age, gender, colour or ethnicity is being led by God according to His specific and unique plan for each of our lives. God formed you very specifically and for a purpose. If you'd like to understand more about finding more of what your life can be, we recommend our free book 'Destiny Living Toolkit' https://www.subscribepage.com/faith-based-living

God's leading will bear fruit in our lives if we co-operate.

That means we decide to follow that leading. Most of the mega-important decisions we take in life come about through many mini-important decisions that we've had to take, so that the big choices become almost second nature to us. The little choices are important because they're set in the context of big convictions. Sometimes, we can see that what we considered to be little decisions are not so little after all. The fruit that Eve ate was small. The red ribbon that Rahab hung in her window was small. The five loaves and the two fishes were insignificant, and yet momentous consequences can come from such small things. That's why we pray about everything.

Prayer: "Lead me today and show me how to grow through Your leading. Help me to listen and watch for Your Spirit and all the ways You'll use to bless me, grow my life and use me."

This is my time

Gideon's victory inspires us to great things. Imagine it - so few daring to go against so many and they win.

It's because God led them step by step and gave His assurance: "By the three hundred men who lapped I will save you, and deliver the Midianites into your hand."

We can learn quite a lot from Gideon that will open a life of great accomplishment to us. So, ask yourself, which of these lessons from Gideon are you applying right now?

-I keep growing in my trust and reliance on God as I hear His instructions.

-I am learning to follow the instructions given me.

-I accept that God's instructions force me out of my comfort zone and are growing me as a leader.

-I am regularly taking time to listen and pray in quiet time with God.

-I expect that my quiet time with God will reveal what's on God's heart.

-I accept that God will lead me in many ways.

-I accept that God leads step by step.

-I know that the small decisions I'm guided to make will build up and have great impact.

-Congratulate yourself for each one you're doing. And make a note of anything above that you need to start doing.

-Next, make a note of which of the channels for God's leading below you're doing and which you're yet to do:

-Prayer
-Fasting
-Praying in tongues
-The Holy Spirit's prompting in my heart
-Bible reading and study
-Gifts of the Spirit - prophecy, word of knowledge and word of wisdom
-Dreams from God
-Visions
-'Thin places'
-Accessing advice from mature, bible-based believers and leaders sensitive to the voice of God.

How did you go?

Did you find yourself smiling that you're already doing many or all of the check points? That's wonderful! Be encouraged because they are blessing your life.

Did you find gaps or something you didn't understand how to use? Take heart that you identified them and can learn about them through reading and through finding mature, practising believers.

Steps I will take

-Each of the checklist points helps you to be led by God opening a life of possibilities to you. You can choose to put into practice the things you noted that you're not yet doing.

-If you're not doing anything because you don't know how, that's fine. You can learn about it through the books we recommended, through church study courses and you can ask God to lead you to where it's practised well.

Coming up

We'll be exploring the ways God leads throughout each chapter. And we'll discover how God will use these ways of leading uniquely in each situation to achieve His objective in our lives.

A Watchful God

"The Lord says, 'I will guide you along the best pathway for your life. I will advise you and watch over you.'" Psalm 32:8-9 NLT.

Excerpt adapted from 'You Are... Uplifting Truths about YOU! Workbook' A Victor.
https://www.amazon.com/author/avictor

One of the most profoundly comforting things about God leading us is that He is ever watchful over us. My partner and I have had many situations in our lives where that watchfulness of God saved our lives or resulted in some miraculous encounter.

Every believer, including you, has this comforting awareness deep within them that God watches over them. The God of all the universe watches over you lovingly He will lead you to take the right action when needed.

This is wonderfully illustrated in the story about John G. Lake, a minister and missionary to Africa. At the time of this story, he was serving in the United States. He was driving up a steep curving road with his wife. Now, if you've ever been to the USA, you'll know that they drive on the right. That's the outer side of the road, closest to the drop.

His Father was watching over him affectionately and kept an eye open for any threats. Suddenly, he heard the voice of God in his heart. This is his account of what now happened in his own words...

'A Voice said, "Pull onto the left of the road and stop."

The left side is the wrong side of the road, and you are breaking the traffic law to be there. But I have listened to that Voice so many years that I have learned in most cases to obey it. Jesus said, "My sheep know my voice." (John 10:27).

(The thought I am trying to bring to you, dear friends, is the value of knowing the Lord and what communion with God means. Salvation is not just something God gives you that is going to bless you after you die; it is having the presence of the Lord now. God has promised to the Christian the guidance and direction of the Holy Spirit).

I pulled onto the left hand side of the road, ran the wheels of my car close into the ditch, and stopped. Immediately, I heard the grinding of a great truck coming around the curve. I had not seen it before. Instead of coming normally, it was coming down the driver's left hand side of the road at a 45 degree angle. The truck had gone out of control and was covering the whole road!

If I had been on my side of the road, it would have sideswiped me and pushed me over the bank. A 100 foot drop down! But I was on the other side when the great thing swept past me. The truck went 50 to 100 feet beyond me, struck a rough spot in the road, and straightened itself. The driver got the truck under control and went on.

Dear friends, men in the Word of God were guided by the Voice of God. God talked to them. This is the inner thing of real Christian experience...'

Pray, listen and respond.

The leading of a loving God is for your benefit and to enlarge your life. God delights in you and is with you as you unfold your life. He's going to give you constant leading, but here's the thing: **You have to listen to what God says, then do something with what He says.**

Although the leading may not be as clear cut as in the story above, **God's leading is taking you somewhere, find out where.** Sometimes God will give a statement that doesn't include a direction or an action. It's up to you to find out what you must do with that leading and what it means.

God often does this to grow your character, resilience and skills. He's building something greater in you as He leads you. He wants you to develop, expand. It's the same intention He had when He set Adam and Eve in the Garden – He gave them opportunity to grow in themselves as they expanded in their knowledge of their surroundings.

You too, are developing, expanding, growing and influencing your surroundings as God leads you. It's part of His plan for you.

Prayer: "Thank you Father, for Your sure and clear leading in all my affairs. I'm listening and ready to respond! I am listening and ready to do what You tell me. I am aware that You are leading my life somewhere and as my life grows, I have to grow too. Thank You for being with me, leading me, in whatever today holds."

This is my time

One of the most comforting things about God leading us is that He's always watchful over us for our good. And so, He will lead you to take the right action as needed.

We read how John G. Lake was kept from plummeting to his death by the leading of our watchful, caring God. Check through these key points from the story to find out if they're in your life...

-I hear the voice of God in my heart and recognise it. "My sheep know my voice." John 10:27.

-I have communion with God and value it.

-I am learning more and more about what communion with God is and how it works.

-I agree that 'Salvation is not just something God

gives you that is going to bless you after you die; it is having the presence of the Lord now... guidance and direction...'

-I agree that being '... guided by the voice of God ... is the inner thing of real Christian experience...'

After the story we covered more key points...

-When I pray, I make sure I also listen and then respond.

-I agree that the constant leading of my loving God is for my benefit and to enlarge my life.

-I accept that God's leading is taking me somewhere. I am to find out where and what I'm to do with that leading.

-I accept that God often leads in a way that develops my character, resilience and skills.

-I agree that God will lead me to transform the world about me for the better. It's part of His plan for me.

How did you go?

Did you find it uplifting as you saw how many things you're already doing and agree with? That's a great encourager!

Did you find gaps? That's good too – you now have the key leading points you can add into your life.

Steps I will take

-Spend time telling God how you value His ever watchful leading in your life.

-Work on any gaps you identified. As you fill them know that you're going to find it easier to flow with God's leading.

Coming up

We are led by our loving God and in turn we are led to lead, God's way...

LED TO LEAD

"Now thanks be to God who always leads us in triumph in Christ, and through us diffuses the fragrance of His knowledge in every place." 2 Corinthians 2:14.

While David was being led by God to the fulfilment of his kingship, he learnt the skills of leadership and people development. He started off his training as a king with those "in distress, everyone who was in debt, and everyone who was discontented gathered to him," and he became captain over them. (1Samuel 22:2). As the story unfolds, we see this small band of unruly men turn into a dedicated and disciplined army as they follow and fight in battle beside him on his journey to the throne.

And David? He grew and matured, just as the men who faithfully followed him. He grew his leadership skills as he met each new challenge with the leading of God. Before great battles and at decision points 'he sought the Lord' and led under the leading of God. And that's why David sought the Lord. He knew he was led by God to lead others and grow towards his kingly destiny.

The result? He sees the fulfilment to what God was leading him toward when the people declare "...you were the one who led Israel out and brought them in; and the Lord said to you, 'You shall shepherd My people Israel, and be ruler over Israel.'" 2 Samuel 5:2.

So, perhaps you're not a king or a Prime Minister or a CEO of a company. It doesn't matter because you're still a leader. You have a sphere of influence where your words and actions impact those around you. And, whether you know it or not, you are influencing and impacting the lives of the people around you.

What is a sphere of influence? It's the circle of people in all aspects of your life that you affect through your decisions and actions. You influence and affect their lives and impact how they live their lives. As an example, on social media platforms, there are 'influencers' who have millions of followers who hang on every word in their posts and imitate their every action. That's their sphere of influence.

Yours may not be as large but you are influencing: your siblings, your children, your partner, your co-workers, your church group and every other area of your life. You do this through actions, words, works and relationships. It's the place you bring your ideas, your guidance, your skills and your talents to influence and to enhance, transform and improve those around you. You're being an influencer in the truest, purest sense of the word.

Follow the Leader.

As believers, we are both leaders and the one who is led. We all have leaders in our lives, people who direct, help and show the way. For example, at work it would be your boss and in sports, it's the coach of the team. Leaders provide a different perspective, experienced counsel and keep you accountable. They also lead you to new heights and assist in you growing your potential. Yet, even the best leaders can only lead so far because as fellow human beings, they too have limited knowledge and capabilities. No earthly leader knows everything.

As a kingdom believer you have the very best, a Leader without limits who "leads us in triumph in Christ." 2 Corinthians 2:14. We are triumphant in living in the power of the Spirit, free from the binding and limiting wrong thinking and wrongdoing. We are constantly led and empowered in the knowledge of God and able to diffuse that to the world around us. We have been given life from heaven, real delight in God, the power of a new affection, and a pure heart, and that causes us to walk as the Spirit directs us. Romans 8:14.

Our Leader gives gifts, waits for us to open them and then leads us on how to use them to expand our lives and change the world.

The loving Spirit walks beside you, guiding you in this moment, giving you the knowledge you need for your life journey. In the leading of God there is a constant flow of gifts given to equip, to grow and to bless you. Like David, you may be growing as a person as you're being led. Or your gift may be the reward for having followed God's leading and seeing the result of you following without wavering. **Whatever form the gifts take in your life, they're there for you to enjoy and use to take you to the next level.**

In the use of the gifts, you co-operate with the leading of the Spirit that you're receiving. You do this by using your skills, talents, gifts and abilities in the way that the Spirit directs. You think. You consider. You act. You make wise judgments. You work out what this leading means in your heart and mind, and then in the home, and in your place of employment, with your neighbours, in your church – wherever God puts you.

Leading like God.

God's leading is all about promoting and growing us. It's not just pointing the way we should go – He's with us every step of the way, fully involved and fully present. And in the way we are led by God we find the way to lead those we have influence over. **God leads to something, equips through gifts, prompts us to open these gifts and leads us into how we should use them. And we use the same pattern in our leading.**

Jesus set up the blueprint of true, affirming leadership when He gave gifts to the church. Here is the purpose for leadership in the church: "So Christ himself gave the apostles, the prophets, the evangelists, the pastors and teachers, to equip his people for works of service, so that the body of Christ may be built up... we will grow to become in every respect the mature body of him who is the head, that is, Christ." Ephesians 4:11-15. NIV.

Jesus' entire focus was that leadership should lead the body of Christ through affirming, upbuilding leadership that grows the individual and releases their gifts and talents. Leadership is also to train those in their care to lead, raising others to lead in maturity and love. This includes every believer in the church being led to grow and expand their lives in a way that brings them joy and delights God.

Opening the gift of your life is all about discovering just what God placed in you. Would you like to know more about some of the spiritual gifts God placed in you and better understand how you think and grow? Do you want to know more about what makes you, well, you? Here's a fun way to discover this that will give you some delightful insights about yourself and the gifts you have.
https://thefluidway.com/wp-content/uploads/2020/08/My-Spiritual-Gifts-Profile.pdf

Prayer: "Help me to copy You as the perfect leader in all the ways I'll lead and influence today. Show me how to create an environment of growth and upliftment for all in my sphere of influence. God, grow my sensitivity to You to understand Your leading and show me how to use my gifts, talents, abilities and resources to touch and transform those in my sphere of influence."

This is my time

While David was being led by God to the fulfilment of his kingship, he grew in the skills of leadership and people development. What can we learn from him?

-No matter what level my leadership skills are right now, I can grow and mature in them with God's guidance.

-My skills grow as I meet each new challenge with the leading of God.

-I accept that I need to be led by God to lead others. Before decisions I will seek the Lord and lead under the leading of God.

-As I'm faithful in being led by God as a leader, others will recognise it.

-I have a sphere of influence - I impact the lives of the people around me. I do this through my actions, words, works and relationships. It's the place I bring my ideas, guidance, skills and talents to influence and to enhance, transform and improve those around me.

-I accept that I am a leader and I'm led. There are leaders in my life who direct, help and show the way.

For example, an employer.

-God as my leader, has full knowledge to share, and gifts for me to open then leads me on how to use them to expand my life and change the world.

-The loving Spirit walks beside me, guiding me in this moment, giving me the knowledge I need for my life journey. In the leading of God there is a constant flow of gifts given to equip, to grow and to bless me.

-I use my skills, talents, gifts and abilities in the way that the Spirit directs and leads.

-I take time to think, consider then act on what God leads me in.

-God's leading is all about promoting and growing me. And I will use the same pattern in leading others.

-I see the blueprint of true leadership in the purpose for leaders in the church - affirming, building, growing each person, releasing their gifts and talents. Leadership also trains those in their care to lead, raising others to lead in maturity and love. See Ephesians 4:11-15.

How did you go?

Did you find that's you're already applying many of the 'Led to Lead' principles already?

Yes. Excellent. You have a basis to grow that leadership ability even more.

No. You are a leader in your sphere of influence already. Allow God's leading to help you develop it, like He did with David.

Steps I will take

-I will take time to consider prayerfully all areas I lead in and how I lead. I have the assurance that as I let God lead me in this, I will develop even further as a leader.

Coming up

Let's see what being led by God to lead looks like in the life of a believer. We'll see him being led by God to lead a violent man to open his gifts and change the world...

A Close Encounter

The Lord said in a vision, "Ananias." And he said, "Here I am, Lord." So the Lord said to him, "Arise and go..." Acts 9:10-11.

Ananias hurried home along the narrow back streets he used as shortcuts. It had been a different fellowship meeting with much discussion around the threat this group of believers faced. Word had gotten around that Saul of Tarsus had arrived in Damascus three days ago bearing letters from the High Priest to use any means to capture believers and return them bound to Jerusalem for judgment of blasphemy. Saul's single-minded hatred of all Christians was well known and deeply feared. They'd heard what had happened to believers that Saul found in Jerusalem. Acts 9:21.

And it was with these thoughts that Ananias arrived at his door and, with one final look up and down the street, slipped inside and closed the door. All the believers in Damascus had much to pray about. They were seeking God's leading on how they could remain steadfast under this new threat and receive deliverance from this evil.

When Ananias rose from his prayer, he felt a cloud had lifted and that God had heard and answered. He wasn't sure how, but he knew it was so. He joined his family for a meal and relaxed into the activity of family time together, enjoying the noise and bustle of his life. Smiling contentedly, he just let it wash over him... and then it happened. Ananias had a vision.

"...the Lord said in a vision, "Ananias." And he said, "Here I am, Lord."

"The Lord said to him, "Arise and go to the street called Straight, and inquire at the house of Judas for one called Saul of Tarsus, for behold, he is praying. "And in a vision he has seen a man named Ananias coming in and putting his hand on him, so that he might receive his sight."

Ananias is devout - he's also logical, knowing Saul's history with believers. He knows it's God leading but has to express what he knows. "Lord, I have heard from many about this man, how much harm he has done to Your saints in Jerusalem. And here he has authority from the chief priests to bind all who call on Your name."

"But the Lord said to him, "Go, for he is a chosen vessel of Mine to bear My name before Gentiles, kings, and the children of Israel."" Ananias knew the vision was true and he knew the voice that spoke to him. God was leading him to lead this enemy of truth to a transformation. Without delay, Ananias hurried to the front door.

God leads to light.

Saul's' heart was changed on the road to Damascus when he encountered the glorified Jesus, and that encounter with the pure light of God left him blind. After his companions had led him to the place he would stay, he sat in his darkness and thought long and hard. His physical blindness emphasised just how blind he had been about Jesus! Gripped with the realisation of what this meant, Saul "was three days without sight, and neither ate nor drank." We can only imagine what this fierce opposer to the truth would have felt and thought in those three long, dark days.

The encounter with God that started on the road to Damascus is about to take Saul to a whole new dimension.

"And Ananias went his way and entered the house; and laying his hands on him he said, "Brother Saul, the Lord Jesus, who appeared to you on the road as you came, has sent me that you may receive your sight and be filled with the Holy Spirit… he received his sight at once; and he arose and was baptized. So when he had received food, he was strengthened. Then Saul spent some days with the disciples at Damascus." Acts 9:1-19.

Saul turned all his passion and knowledge of God to perfecting his understanding. He is on the mission of his life. Having been led by Ananias to the truth, he opens the gift of truth he's been given and with God's help and the leading of the believers in Damascus, learns how to use it.

Our takeaway.

How Ananias responded to the vision and the actions he took all serve as an example to us. Visions can be tricky, especially if they lead you into dangerous and life-threatening situations. But Ananias was versed in God and how He worked and knew it was a true vision. He had a strong, comfortable relationship with God that allowed him to speak freely of his concerns in obeying. Ananias was obviously led and loved by God, so God expands the reason Saul must be ministered to. God shares His plan for Saul with Ananias.

In following the leading of God, you will discover a widening world of knowledge about what God is doing – not only in your life but in the lives of others and the world. God's leading takes you somewhere – there's action involved. And in the taking you somewhere you will witness and experience many wonderful and marvellous things. There are amazing sights to see, things to achieve, places to explore, experiences to grow and expand you.

Ananias was given part of God's plan for Saul, Israel and the Gentiles. **Having knowledge through God's leading emboldens you to take the actions in God's leading.** You understand you are part of a plan unfolding, there's purpose in the discomfort or risk or change you are about to face. But because you know the plan you can bolster your courage and act.

Without delay, Ananias went to fulfil God's leading. He had accepted the mandate of God, knew the plan and spoke in boldness and authority, knowing He is under the leading of God. He's God's representative. The result is Saul is instantly healed. When we accept the leading of God we can operate in the authority of faith, knowing we are spot on with God and so we expect miracles.

Without reservation, Ananias accepts Saul, fully accepting that God had changed him and will now use him. When God places us with people with 'histories', it may be difficult to change our behaviour to them. That's why in situations like these it's so important to find healing for yourself and forgiveness for the other person. Forgiveness doesn't mean forgetting, it means choosing how you'll remember the hurt. God put aside what Saul had done and chose Saul to lead many to Christ.

The leading of Ananias.

Ananias was one of the believers, he held no special place in the community of believers, yet God chose him to be the vessel through which Saul receives his sight and a confirmation of his ministry. Ananias listened to God's leading, responded to what he heard by following through with the required action. He used the leading of God to, in turn, lead Saul to truth.

In all the God's leading in your life, He'll use you to lead others to transformation. It may not be as dramatic as Ananias', but you'll be changing people's lives in ways only you, uniquely, can. As God wants you to grow in yourself and your relationship with Him, He'll lead you at times to stretch and grow – just like Ananias had to trust and go.

Prayer: "I want to hear Your voice today and know more through visions and Your voice guiding me to bring transformation to myself and others. Give me boldness to answer Your leading and do what You tell me, even the difficult things. Empower me with Your Spirit to flow in the miraculous in what You lead me to do."

This is my time

In the story of Paul's and Ananias we find many valuable lessons on God's leading (Acts 9:1-20). It's well worthwhile spending time studying this as there are such rich details on God leading. It can help us rise to new levels of expectancy in our walk with God.

Check the key factors below:

-Physical manifestation - light so bright it blinded.

-Conversations in which God gives very detailed instructions and information including things in the future, response, further clarification, call to action.

-Prayer with fasting.

-Physically blind, Saul has a vision in which he hears the name Ananias and is shown the future – Ananias will lay his hand on him and his sight is to be restored.

-Ananias treats Saul as a fellow believer which he is.

-Saul spending time with other believers and then publicly share what he now knows.

All of these are ways that God can lead you. Now, in view of the above check these key points out. Note your responses:

-I am expectant that God will communicate to me in various ways including visions.

-I am comfortable in my relationship with God and speak to him respectfully and in a normal way like Ananias.

-I listen for His response, instructions and details.

-I am able to voice my concerns with God who already knows my thoughts.

-I accept that as I follow the leading of God, I will discover a widening world of knowledge about what God is doing – not only in your life but in the lives of others and the world.

-God's leading involves actions I must take.

-I understand that I'm part of God's plans and it helps me to take courage, like Ananias.

-I act without delay once it's clear what God leads me to do.

-I have expectancy that what he tells me to do will happen, like Ananias laying his hand on Saul to restore his sight.

-Like Ananias accepting that Saul is fully changed I treat people who come to God as born again fellow disciples who are growing in right ways.

-I accept that God's leading in my life means that He'll use me to lead others to transformation.

-I accept that God wants me to grow in myself and my relationship with Him.

How did you go?

Leading like we saw with Saul and Ananias is not an everyday thing. Even so, did you identify with any of their experiences?

Yes? Be encouraged. God's leading is a precious gift.

Did you have gaps? That's to be expected. As you keep on developing your experience of God's leading, you'll find more and more of His range of leading in your life.

Steps I will take

-I will study biblical examples of God's leading. And prayerfully seek to be open to God's leading and ask him to help me grow in it.

Coming up

You're ready to go on this great adventure with God. Is God doing all the planning for your life journey and what are you supposed to do? Let's explore...

SHOULD I HAVE LIFE PLANS IF I'M LED BY GOD?

"I Know the plans I have for you, declares the Lord, plans for welfare and not for evil, to give you a future and a hope." Jeremiah 29:11.

Excerpt adapted from 'GOALS Christian Journal and Planner'
https://www.amazon.co.uk/dp/1915349079

From the moment of creation, we see God, the great Planner, in action. He's a God of plans. He planned a perfect environment for the first humans before He created them. He planned the Garden of Eden to be a place where they could expand in the knowledge of themselves, their environment and God. When they lost their way, He had a plan in place already - a way back to Him through the cross, in this life and beyond.

So, as God always has a plan, we shouldn't really plan, right? Wrong.

We are creative beings, just like God, and the desire to create is built into us by our Creator. In order to create you must have a clear idea of what you are about to make, whatever it is. For example, if you build a house, you have to think about who will live in it, what they'll need and how to make the house suited to them because you're creating an environment for them. You have to have a detailed plan drawn up of the building and then you'd have to build the house according to the plan.

I realise building a house is more complicated than the few points I mentioned, but it does illustrate the point: there must be a well thought out plan before you create anything. That applies to your life as well.

God made you with a specific plan in mind.

God made you unique in every way, from your fingerprints and DNA right down to how you think, learn and view the world. God is in the business of creating originals and He'll use you uniquely and will lead you uniquely, just like He did with Jeremiah.

This is how God reveals that Jeremiah is unique with a definite calling: "I knew you before I formed you in your mother's womb. Before you were born I set you apart and appointed you as my prophet to the nations." Jeremiah 1:5 NLT.

God's plan for Jeremiah's life comes with God's guarantee of leading and God gives these assurances:
-Direction and confirmation - "Don't say, 'I'm too young,' for you must go wherever I send you and say whatever I tell you."
-Safety and assurance - "And don't be afraid of the people, for I will be with you and will protect you."
-Equipped and anointed - "Then the Lord reached out and touched my mouth and said, "Look, I have put my words in your mouth!"

God's plan for your life will also have tangible assurances to enable you to step where He leads through His plan and to bear fruit through it. You'll find out more as you spend time with God and as you do what God leads you to do. Success comes through your willingness to follow His leading by listening and then doing what He tells you to do. God's plans always bear fruit – there's some tangible result.

Big picture and small steps.

That's the grand life picture, but what about your day to day living and the desires you have? "The heart of man plans his way, but the Lord establishes his steps." Proverbs 16:9. God loves it when you take the gifts, talents and abilities He's given you and expand them – it's a form of honouring your loving Creator. By finding the desires that fit with what you were made to be, you can plan and do in co-operation with God to see your dreams fulfilled.

So, by all means, have plans and set goals, get that academic degree, start a family, open a business or whatever your heart desires. Once you've prayed and listened, ask these questions:

- Can I see where I need to jog and where I need to sprint in this? Can I identify the different long-term and short-term goals I have in place?
- Are these in line with my faith and values?
- How will they impact my loved ones?

Paul understood the difference between his life mission given by God and the goals he set to fulfil his vision of growing the faith. "So I run with purpose in every step. I am not just shadowboxing. I discipline my body like an athlete, training it to do what it should." 1 Corinthians 9:26-27.

We can see examples of Paul's planning and God's planning in harmony in the bible:

Paul tells the believers in Rome about his plan to visit them on his way somewhere: "Whensoever I take my journey into Spain, I will come to you..."

Here, the Spirit doesn't tell him he won't be going to Spain. Circumstances does that. In the next example the Spirit had prevented them from concluding their plan. He informed them not to go to the province of Asia as He had other plans: "Now when they had gone through Phrygia and the region of Galatia, they were forbidden by the Holy Spirit to preach the word in (the province) of Asia." Acts 16:6.

So, we see that an experienced believer like Paul put purpose and discipline into his planning so he could grow the churches and expand his ministry. And he was sensitive to the Spirit's directives to adjust his plans to align with God's plans.

So, yes, plan and be sensitive to God's instructions.

You were created to expand, create, grow, learn, have fun, and use your sphere of influence to make the world around you a better place. God made you to work toward goals. It's impossible to run a race without knowing how far you'll be running and the structure of the race. 1 Corinthians 9:26 shows Paul lived and ministered with vision and purpose and planning. You have to plan the pace of your life, knowing when to sprint and when to jog.

Waiting on God is not inaction.

God is leading your life every day and you have to take steps every day by following His leading. God reveals and leads a few steps at a time. He expects us to take the steps that He reveals while we live our lives and expand ourselves. To be led, you must take the steps, the actions needed. God takes your hand but you have to actually walk to be led.

A woman I knew came to me very upset after a prophetic service. She had gone looking for a word from God. The prophet looked at her and simply said, 'You are waiting on God, but God is waiting on you.' She had spent years in prayer and confession without any personal action and it had resulted in little personal growth and no plan to expand her life. Her inaction had brought her life to personal and financial ruin and God was gently pointing her to the fact that she had to take charge of her life.

We each are given this amazing gift of life by a

loving God. His gift of your life is filled with talents, abilities and all manner of wonderful 'extras' added by a God who delights in you and what you'll do with this gift of life. Like any gift, you must open the gift to discover what it is, then use it and enjoy it.

I've counselled many believers over the years who have fallen into the same wrong habit through wrong teaching or simply not doing anything. They will often say they don't want to do something wrong, so they do nothing. I remind them that to learn to walk they had to fall a few times before they got it right.

If you keep God in the plans and desires you are working on, His Spirit will lead you to course correct when you are veering off the road. God knows you intimately, knows all the gifts and talents He placed in you. By letting Him take the lead through the Spirit, you're guaranteed success!

Making the right plans.

So, how do you know if what you're planning is acceptable to God? Jeremiah 29:11 states God plans are always for good and not for evil and they give you a future and a hope. It helps to always ask yourself if the plans you're making for your family, for others and yourself are in line with this.

It can be hard to clarify *how* to plan and *what* to plan, especially if you want to please God. To assist you in this, I've created a God centred Journal specially designed for success-minded Christians. I've distilled all my experience in Christian Ministry, Business and my practical Training in Psychology and Counselling to bring you a powerful, effective, and fun goalsetting system that will bring you results as you follow the prompts. It's Spirit focussed, biblical and full of uplifting scripture and positive statements. So, you'll be creating the right environment spiritually and mentally as you allow your creative brain to effectively assist the effort you put into achieving your goals. https://www.amazon.co.uk/dp/1915349079

Prayer: "Thank You, Loving Creator, for making me unique and for the special plan you have for my life. Show me the steps I need to take to follow Your leading today. Give me witty inventions and help me use my talents, gifts and skills to grow my life through actions that will please you and benefit myself and others."

This is my time

God's the great Planner and you're a planner too. Go through each statement below and note which are in your life and which need your attention. This will help you to achieve greater success in your plans.

The big picture of my life:

-I accept that God made me unique, with a specific plan in mind. God gives His assurance that He'll lead me and equip me in what I'm to do in His plans for me.

-As God has a plan for my life I spend time with God listening and then doing what God leads me to do.

-I know that success comes through following God's leading as His plans always have tangible results.

The day to day steps in my life:

-I understand that in my day to day living, I'll have desires. I'll plan to achieve them and God will help and guide me. "The heart of man plans his way, but the Lord establishes his steps." Proverbs 16:9.

-I accept that I can have my own plans and set goals e.g. what to study for a career I chose, starting a family, opening a business or whatever my heart desires.

-Once I've prayed and listened, I ask questions:

-Can I see what pace I need to take in this?

-Can I identify the long-term and short-term goals I have in place?

-Are these in line with my faith and values?

-How will they impact my loved ones and others?

-I understand that an experienced believer like Paul had a life plan from God and he made his own plans too. When needed God will tell you to course correct.

-I plan and ensure that I stay sensitive to God's instructions.

-I accept that God made me to work toward goals, a vision, a purpose. To do this well, I plan – I consider the pace I need to go at and the steps I need to take.

-When I'm waiting on God for his leading, I don't fall into inaction. I accept that I'll make mistakes. That's normal, and I don't let this stop me from starting.

-I know that God's leading my life every day and I have to take steps every day by following His leading.

-I know that God reveals and leads a few steps at a time. I take the steps He reveals.

-God knows me intimately, knows all the gifts and talents He placed in me. So, I let Him take the lead through the Spirit - this guarantees my success.

-As I keep God in the plans and desires I'm working on, His Spirit leads me to course correct when I'm veering off track.

-To make the right plans, I check to see if what I'm planning is acceptable to God. I do this by regularly asking myself the following: is the plan I'm making for my family, for others and myself going to result in good outcomes? What can I anticipate will be the result?

How did you go?

In the big picture of your life and in your daily life did you find you were doing many of the key points?

If so, you have a solid foundation of planning that

will help you succeed.

If not, adding more structure is going to bless you and your sphere of influence.

Steps I will take

-Take your 'I'm doing this' list and take time to appreciate how this has been helping you.

-Plan to set in place those things you saw were missing. Then enjoy the benefits.

Coming up

We should plan and work towards fulfilling the desires of our heart. But there are many choices and many directions you can take. As God gives you choices in how you invest your life, how do you know which path in life is the best for you? Let's explore...

FINDING YOUR PATH AND YOUR SONG

"Show me Your ways, Lord, teach me Your paths. Guide me in Your truth and teach me, for You are God my Saviour, and my hope is in You all day long." Psalm 25:4-5.

Excerpt adapted from 'GIFTS for Destiny and Life'
https://www.amazon.co.uk/dp/1838021000

Exploring the two life questions we all face: Who am I? and Why am I here? Ever asked yourself these questions when pondering the big questions of life and the meaning of life - the 'what's it all about?' questions? It's wired into our self-awareness to want to understand this, like an embedded core program deep within ourselves needing to be explored. Deep down in every person, there's a knowing that we were born for a reason. We have things to achieve, a legacy to leave behind that'll make the world better. There's a compulsion to move and expand and grow.

So, is a purposeful life or destiny living some profound, single, higher purpose that we must make our mission to find? Or do we just live for a time, do some important things that give us meaning and make us feel good and some things that don't?

Healthy forms of questioning can lead to many discoveries about yourself, but it can also pull you into a never-ending loop of feeling overwhelmed by it all and not doing anything because you're not sure what to do. That's why your time with God and the assurance in your heart that you are led are so important.

God never thinks small things of His creation. By His very nature, He is abundant, dynamic, loving and giving and has given you abundant life through Jesus John 10:10. The simplest way to honour God is by you living and enjoying the fullness of everything given. But it can be overwhelming. What do you do with all you've been given and how do you use it to find your path in life?

Be real.

God made you specifically and He wants you to be what He made you for, and that will be unique to you. You are a purposefully and carefully thought out creation. Psalm 139:16. God wants you to live in truth because it's only in truth that you'll find God. That includes your path in life. So, don't follow a career, a life, a ministry because others have told you that's the way you should go. Also don't assume someone else's vision as your ultimate path. By all means, give your talents and time to grow the vision your boss has for his business and leadership has for the ministry – BUT don't let that be the defining path of your life.

Authenticity is at the heart of everything that truly matters. When you live your true self, living becomes easier, and people, seeing who you actually are, find inspiration in your honesty. **You, being you, often inspires the person you're with to be them, creating an upward spiral of truth in living that will change their lives and your relationship.**

Your path is a journey, not a destination.

All the gifts in you and around you become tools of empowerment only when you know about them and understand how to use them. This should not be scary to you or make you feel under obligation, it's exciting! You're opening the gift of life you were given. Knowing more about yourself is a way to know more about God.

How? **By seeing what potential was placed in you by your Creator and actually deciding to release and live it will give you a new appreciation of just how much you mean to God.** The image and likeness of God in you finds expression through you in the life you live. So, inner exploration is a huge treasure hunt!

God leads in steps; you are walking together. In looking at Jeremiah, we see God always releases (Jeremiah 1:9-10) what He implanted (Jeremiah 1:5), although we may resist it. The potential placed in the unformed mass of Jeremiah in the womb is now drawn out and released by God at the appointed time when Jeremiah is ready. Knowing that this is what God does, ask Him boldly what He had in mind when He made you so your life may be abundant and be the blessing to the world it was intended to be.

You were created with purpose in every part of you. Even as an unformed mass in your mother's womb you already had a unique purpose and a lifespan. Psalm 139:16. God thought out your potential and abilities before you were even formed. He thought about how you should be and what you should be and put in the perfect blend of gifts, talents, abilities, and capabilities in you for you to develop, grow and stretch into your potential. **Then He gave you free will to choose how much you will allow of that in your life.** And because you are a joint heir with Jesus, He also gave His own Spirit to empower, comfort and guide you through life and living as you live out the choices you made.

Don't try and figure out your whole life today. Make your long term plans, set your goals, listen to God's leading and do what is in front of you today. It's a great way to stay in the present, grow and live in today, in your life and your relationships. Above all, enjoy the abundance of the gift of life.

Significance and a man named pain.

Your significance to God does not depend on where you are, whether you are rich or poor, black or white, have a disability or a chequered past. **He is leading you and looks at what you are becoming.**

1 Chronicles 4:9-10 "Now Jabez (pain, sorrowful) was more honourable than his brothers, and his mother called his name Jabez, saying, 'Because I bore him in pain'. And Jabez called on the God of

Israel saying, 'Oh that You would bless me indeed, and enlarge my territory, that Your hand would be with me and that You would keep me from evil, that I may not cause pain.' So, God granted him what he requested." What a simple end statement to spectacular blessing. Jabez had spent his life living a story. He was the man called pain. But he did not allow that to define who he was or the largeness of his life. He changed his story.

No matter what story you or others have made about you, the story can change, and should, because you are God's own and He is leading you. "...for it is God who works in you both to will and to do for His good pleasure." Philippians 2:13.

We have often faced this question of purpose in our work in teaching, counselling, and coaching when dealing with someone who wants to release more potential in their lives or with others who feel they can't get started. We have met many highly gifted people who end up in a loop trying to find meaning in living but who seem dissatisfied with the results of their lives. Why does this happen? Let's start with this basic:

It's all in the question and the perception.

Let me explain. **You might not have found something that makes you feel your life has meaning because you're asking the wrong questions.** Think about the questions you asked about this. Are they something like: 'What should I do in life?' or 'What is life purpose?' Yes? Here are a few far better questions to ask: (Please write out your answers so you can refer to them later in prayer. Writing them makes it more tangible).

•Instead of asking 'What is the meaning of life?' personalise it and ask, 'What is the meaning of my life?' Putting focus on yourself will give you an opportunity to dig below the surface and ask more specific questions. This will help you understand your values, talents, and potential.

Some people come up with a blank, some get a vague idea, and some get something very definite. Whichever category you fall into, ask:

•'What is important to me?' This includes your values, what you believe is important about others and the world.

•'What am I truly good at?' This includes your talents and what you're passionate about.

•'What do I want to become right now?' Life is full of choices. Do you want to chart a new course, grow, or change in an area? Think what you'd really like (not what others would like for you).

If you're multi-functional (like Leonardo Da Vinci), you'll have a great deal that appeals to you and that you're passionate about. You'll not want to limit your life to just one area and you'll enjoy different things. If you're a specialist (like Einstein), you'll want to choose one trajectory and build your life on it. It will be important for you that all your knowledge and work leads to enhancing this central theme of your life. It's just about understanding how you are wired and realising destiny living is fluid, growing and expanding all the time.

•'How can I invest my life to make a difference?' This question brings you to where you are, what you have right now and how you can use it. It's a moment by moment thing where you are conscious and living your life, in this moment, just like Jesus lived His life while on earth. Many people we have worked with feel they don't have anything going right now, but that's not true. No matter how old or young you are, you have already used some of your skills and talents and you have experienced relationships and other 'stuff' that makes up living. You learnt things while experiencing these things and performing these tasks. You've also learnt some things about yourself.

Write down your answers to the above and anything else that comes to mind (good or bad). This is you talking to you and allowing yourself the space to discover where you want to go and what matters to you.

So, what did you learn about yourself? A lot? Not so much? Either way is great, because this is an amazing journey of discovery you and God are taking together. "I will instruct you and teach you in the way you should go; I will counsel you with my loving eye on you." Psalm 32:8-9.

Your path is in the patterns.

There are patterns in your life - re-occurring events, themes and or failures. You also have talents and this 'thing' that drives your passion. The 'stuff' you have a 'knack' with. That's part of your path. Once you start to pay attention to the themes that run through your life you find the same themes appearing at distinct and measurable intervals. Upon closer inspection you will find the notes within the themes and begin to discern the melody of the song your life.

Training your life to sing your song.

As you learn to listen to your life song, you identify those notes that are discordant to your song and learn to flow in the song of your life. The notes are drawn out from the inside of you to form the melody and life you will live outwardly. **With each note you discover why you are here, and in the melody of your song, you discover your destiny.** You trade in your picture and beliefs about yourself and others for the real self that no longer conforms to the image of the world. How? Through programming your mind for living in your Creator's full plan for your life.

The full beauty of your life and your magnificent song is revealed as you draw the hidden notes out of yourself through the self-discovery of training and growing. Anything that is effective in life has a result it works toward. Success needs a goal. And a goal must have a plan.

You are finely tuned and magnificently made. Michelangelo puts it this way, 'The more the marble wastes, the more the statue grows.' By chiselling away the edges, the unformed block of stone starts taking on the shape of the statue - the unformed mass takes on the form of beauty. **Just like the marble chips away to allow the emergence of the beautiful statue, the chipping away of those limiting patterns that encase your life allow the real you to emerge and your song can be sung fully.**

Weave the song of your life with your Creator. **He wants you to sing together with Him over your life.** "...The mighty One will save, He will rejoice over you with gladness, He will quiet you with His love, He will rejoice over you with singing."

If you're ready to take this adventure of your life further, I have combined all my experience in helping others find their path in life in two books.
'GIFTS for Destiny and Life'
https://www.amazon.co.uk/dp/1838021000
'The Bridge of Possibility: How to link the physical and the spiritual to release your destiny'
https://www.amazon.co.uk/dp/B07Z787J3H

Prayer: "Thank You for loving me as much as you love Jesus and giving me an abundant life. Show me how to sing my life song with You. Help me to deal with the limitations I've set on *my life and move into the fullness You have for me. Lead me as I take the steps and walk beside You."*

This is my time

-I have an assurance in my heart that I was born for a reason. I have things to achieve, a legacy to leave behind that will make the world better.

-I believe that God made me specifically and He wants me to be what He made me for and that it will be unique to me.

-I will avoid following a career, a life, a ministry because others have told me that's the way I should go. And I won't assume someone else's vision as my ultimate path.

-When I give my talents and time to grow the vision of an employer boss or a leader in ministry, I won't let that be the defining path of my life.

-I accept that God will lead me in steps, as we walk together. I won't try and figure out my whole life today.

-I'm asking Him boldly what He had in mind when He made me so my life may be abundant and be the blessing to the world it was intended to be.

-I understand that God gave me free will and He also gave His Spirit to empower, comfort and guide me through life as I live out the choices I make.

-I'm making my long term plans, setting my goals, listening to God's leading and doing what's in front of me today.

-I know that my significance has nothing to do with circumstances of any kind. Like Jabez, 1 Chronicles 4:9-10, I can call on the God saying, '... bless me indeed, and enlarge my territory, that Your hand would be with me and keep me from evil, that I may not cause pain.'

-I accept that no matter what my story has been, it can change, and should, because I am God's own and He is leading me.

-In the section entitled 'It's all in the question and the perception' I will check that I asked myself all the questions and made notes of what I learnt about myself.

How did you go?

Whether you've learnt a lot more or just a little about yourself, it adds to the amazing journey of discovery you and God are taking together. He'll continue to instruct, teach and counsel you in the way you should go Psalm 32:8-9.

Steps I will take

-I'll look for the patterns in my life that form the path I'm taking. I'll pay attention to the themes that run through my life and the notes within the themes and I'll begin to discern the melody of the song your life.

Then I'll be able to identify those notes that are discordant to my song, discard them and learn to flow in the song of my life.

Coming up

It's great singing your song and walking with God in the happy times when you're sure of things and all feels well. But what about the times where you're not feeling God or times of uncertainty? Meet an ordinary man hiding in a winepress who's about to change a nation...

CLARITY AND COURAGE

"Commit your way to the Lord; trust in Him, and He will act." Psalm 37:5.

Desperate times call for desperate measures, that's what Gideon thought. And these were desperate times indeed. For seven years, Israel had been ruthlessly oppressed by the Midianites. "They would come up with their livestock and their tents, coming in as numerous as locusts; both they and their camels were without number; and they would enter the land to destroy it." Judges 6:5. In order to save their family's livelihood and food source, Gideon and his father devised a plan: they threshed their wheat in their winepress. It's the only way they could hide their food from the raiding Midianites.

And so, on one hot day we find Gideon threshing. He stopped for a moment and wiped his brow. He still had much to do but he needed a rest. A sudden movement under the terebinth tree caught his eye. "And the Angel of the Lord appeared to him, and said to him, "The Lord is with you, you mighty man of valour!"

Gideon is a practical man, living under heavy oppression. He has not seen a mighty God or known the miracles of old. He's struggling to feed his family with no relief in sight. He's not moved by this sudden appearance of an angel in his winepress. He's quite direct in his challenge. Unfazed by the fact that he's facing heaven's messenger, he replies, "O my Lord, if the Lord is with us, why then has all this happened to us? And where are all His miracles which our fathers told us about, saying, 'Did not the Lord bring us up from Egypt?' But now the Lord has forsaken us and delivered us into the hands of the Midianites."

Have you ever been at this place in your life? You've seen or heard of God's leading in mighty ways and yet you're caught in a situation where you see neither leading nor deliverance. It's a place we all experience at some time or another in our lives, whether we've known God's great miracles and leading or not. In that 'stuck' place it's hard to see how to move forward. **The thing about 'stuck' places is that the longer you are stuck, the more it becomes habit, the norm, and the harder it is to become unstuck.**

Choice and change.

God knows this and will usually lead you out of that stuck place with an event, a happening – something to wake you out of the daily grind habit. But you have free will – you will choose to follow God's leading or not. It will mean change for you and in you and you will have to choose to make the change, committing yourself to what God is leading you into.

You're going into an unknown situation, untested waters, and it's normal to feel uncertain. Let's face it, it's a little scary. Being grounded and established in prayer and secure in God's leading is going to lead you through. And in situations like this, the best place to be is up close and personal with God, listening and waiting for His leading.

Back to Gideon and the Angel of the Lord...

Gideon is about to be faced with a life changing choice. "Then the Lord said, "Go in this might of yours, and you shall save Israel from the hand of the Midianites. Have I not sent you?" Gideon is slow to be convinced or to be moved by this great declaration. "Then he said to Him, "If now I have found favour in Your sight, then show me a sign that it is You who talk with me."

Gideon prepares a sacrifice and under the instruction of the Angel lays the unleavened bread and meat on the rock and pours the broth over it. "Then the Angel of the Lord put out the end of the staff that was in His hand, and touched the meat and the unleavened bread; and fire rose out of the rock and consumed the meat and the unleavened bread. And the Angel of the Lord departed out of his sight."

Gideon is terrified! He has seen the Lord in a time where there was little evidence of miracles and God seemed very distant. A loving God makes allowances for this and comforts him. Then the Lord said to him,

"Peace be with you; do not fear, you shall not die." God has awakened Gideon to a new level of being led. He is willing but not yet experienced in this new level of leading.

Gideon is a changed man through this encounter, ready to obey but still not sure how. God instructs him to tear down the altar to Baal and the image beside it and erect an altar to God in its place. He goes at night because he fears the men of the city and his father. **He's learning to obey and his conviction in his choices are growing stronger.** Gideon is growing under the leading of God with every choice he makes that moves him out of his comfort zone.

God takes it to the next level.

God's leading now places Gideon as leader to begin to fulfil his calling. This is a whole new level. Ever been here? God asks you to do something so far beyond what you're accustomed to or, in your thinking, capable of. You, just like Gideon, are faced with a choice. What will you need to motivate you to make the right choice? Gideon asked for yet another sign.

God meets each situation in a unique way.

You know what's coming. Yep, the fleece. The Midianites and Amalekites come up and Gideon seeks reassurance from God. He puts out a fleece for two nights and ask God to use it as a sign. God responds and Gideon prepares to fight the Midianites.

For Gideon, God had to lead him into trusting, like a little child, giving him one final assurance before he would fulfil his destiny. Judges 7:13 God tells Gideon to go to the camp of the Midianites where he overhears a man sharing his dream. "I have had a dream: To my surprise, a loaf of barley bread tumbled into the camp of Midian; it came to a tent and struck it so that it fell and overturned, and the tent collapsed. Then his companion answered and said, "This is nothing else but the sword of Gideon! Into his hand God has delivered Midian and the whole camp. And so it was, when Gideon heard the telling of the dream and its interpretation, that he worshiped. He returned to the camp of Israel, and said, "Arise, for the Lord has delivered the camp of Midian into your hand."

Many sincere believers have used 'the fleece' to 'confirm' choices or decisions. The young woman who has a major crush on a less than ideal man who prays 'If he walks past my window, I'll know I should marry him.' Or the man who just sits and prays without providing for his family, waiting for God to 'confirm' his ministry.

These are extreme and absurd examples I'm using from real life that we've encountered. I used them to show up what happens when this type of thinking is used to confirm your next action. God allowed this with Gideon because he had not seen the miracles of God. But we, as believers, know the power of God. We are born again, filled with the Spirit who leads in all truth and have the evidence of signs, wonders and miracles. We also have prayer, mature leaders in the church to guide us and just simple common sense.

Just as God led Gideon specifically in the way he needed to bring him to action, God will be leading your life in many different ways every day. As you walk beside Him, He will show the way you should go. If you are praying about starting a new business, God is not also going to tell you to become a full time medical missionary in a remote part of the bush. So, it's important for us to approach how God leads us with thinking and logic as well as prayer and Spirit, and let go of any confirmation bias we have.

Prayer: "Lord, I declare I will endeavour to live Psalm 37. I will trust You; I will do good and be faithful. I will delight myself in You and walk by Your side and You will give me the desires of my heart. I have committed my way to You, You establish This is my time and You act on my behalf."

This is my time

Hiding their food, Gideon's threshing wheat in secret. In contradiction to the seeming evidence the Angel of the Lord called him "... mighty man of valour." He replies negatively, "... if the Lord is with us, why? ... the Lord has forsaken us..."

We identified this as Gideon being in a 'stuck' place.

We all, at some time, experience this.

-Take time to think, are there 'stuck places' in your life, at this time? If so, what are they?

Gideon is faced with a life changing choice when he's told, "Go in this might of yours, and you shall save Israel from the hand of the Midianites. Have I not sent you?" He's still negative and asks, "If now I have found favour ... show me a sign."

-Are there things in your thinking that contradict what God has told you? If so, make note of them and set out what God has told you about each, in the bible, in your heart and through other leading.

God takes Gideon to new levels of being led step by step. He still wants a sign.

-We are born again, have the leading of the Spirit and close relationship with God. So, we trust, through experience what God leads us into, rather than relying on signs.

-I accept that I am to approach how God leads me with thinking, logic and common sense as well as prayer and His guidance.

How did you go?

Did you find any 'stuck places' in your current thinking?

No? That's great. You can flow with God's leading unhindered.

Yes? That's great too. You now know what you can unblock with God's leading.

Steps I will take

-Thank God for all the things you're flowing in right now.

-If you identified one or more 'stuck places', thank God that with His guidance you'll take action to remove any blocks.

-Go over the chapter to encourage yourself, pray and listen for solutions.

Coming up

One of the wonderful ways God leads is through our dreams. We're about to visit a carpenter who through a dream must let go of his own confirmation bias to take on his mission in life...

CONVERSATIONS OF THE NIGHT

"...the angel of the Lord appeared to him in a dream, saying, 'Joseph, son of David, do not be afraid to take Mary as your wife." Matthew 1:20

Excerpt adapted from 'God's 'Thin Places"
https://www.amazon.co.uk/dp/B09XLLCFVL
and 'Tales out of Africa: Ordinary People having Extraordinary Encounters with God'
https://www.amazon.co.uk/dp/B0957GZKMP

Joseph was excited. Mary, his future bride, was back home. It had been three long months since he last saw her. He had missed her very much since her sudden decision to visit her relative Elizabeth. He'd hardly had time to say goodbye before she hurried off and she seemed both excited and distracted at their parting.

Anyway, none of that mattered now. Mary was back and he was going to see her today. He had used these last three months to prepare for their coming marriage and couldn't wait to tell Mary about it. Turning the corner he saw Mary sitting alone under the tree in front of her house. Strange, he thought, that the family is not around her catching up on all the news.

Mary rose smiling and uncertain, her face strained. 'Joseph! I have to tell you something wonderful.' His smile froze on his face as he looked at her swollen belly...

We can only imagine that first conversation Mary had with Joseph. It could not have been easy for either of them. And although Joseph did not yet know it, God would lead him to become the protector of the Saviour of the world and Mary. That's quite a mission to wrap your head around, even for a devout and law abiding man.

God has a plan.

God is leading Joseph into action, it's a personal and directed leading to ensure a specific outcome. "But while he thought about these things, an angel of the Lord appeared to him in a dream, saying, "Joseph, son of David, do not be afraid to take to you Mary your wife, that which is conceived in her is of the Holy Spirit."

At times it takes a dream to get us into the right mental state of awareness to perceive God's leading. There's a very good reason for this built into your amazing brain. Your brain is an electrochemical organ and electrical activity emanating from the brain is displayed in the form of brainwaves. There are four categories of these brainwaves, ranging from the most activity to the least activity, but we're focusing on Theta waves that happen just as you go to sleep or wake up.

In Theta you are deeply relaxed, and your brain is in 'creative' brain time where you are functioning on an open, receptive mode. You are meditative, relaxed and flexible and your thinking is 'bigger.' It's when you get good ideas and solve problems – answers coming after you sleep on it. So, Joseph had been prepared and was receptive with the right mental set to move beyond his thinking boundaries into the extraordinary.

Dreams are used by God with Joseph specifically to bring him to definite actions. A while after the birth of Jesus, Joseph has another dream to guide him in his role as the protector of the Saviour of the world. "An angel of the Lord appeared to Joseph in a dream, saying, "Arise, take the young Child and His mother, flee to Egypt, and stay there until I bring you word; for Herod will seek the young Child to destroy Him." When he arose, he took the young Child and His mother by night and departed for Egypt." Matthew 2:13-14. Joseph acted on what God instructed him in his dreams to keep Jesus and Mary safe.

God has always led through dreams and uses dreams to instruct, warn or transform the dreamer. The three wise men who followed the Star to bring gifts and worship Jesus "being divinely warned in a dream that they should not return to Herod, they departed for their own country another way." Mark 2:12. And we experienced many dreams that saved our lives while ministering in war torn areas. We share some of these and more about dreams in our book 'Tales out of Africa: Ordinary people having Extraordinary Encounters with God.' https://www.amazon.co.uk/dp/B0957GZKMP

The point of dreaming.

"For God speaks in one way, and in two, though man does not perceive it. In a dream, in a vision of the night, when deep sleep falls on men, while they slumber on their beds." Job 33:14-15.

Dreams are the range of stories and images that your mind creates when you sleep. It's a different state of consciousness with definite brainwave activity. Dreaming is a necessary and wonderful part of being alive. In this unique state of consciousness, experiences of the present, processing of the past, and preparation of the future take place. Dreams can also delve into unconscious desires and wishes or unresolved issues. And sometimes a dream is simply the interpretation of random signals from the brain and body during sleep, like dreaming about water when you have a full bladder.

So, how do we understand our dreams? How do we know what to do with our dreams? Get to know yourself – record your dreams in a dream journal, talk about them and think about them. **Treat your dreams as a valid tool to enhance your life and a way that God will lead you.**

God uses your dreams to speak to you, direct you, reveal destiny and prospering and warn you and wants you to take note, Habakkuk 2:2. Daniel also understood the importance of writing and understanding a dream or vision and acting on it, Daniel 7:1. **God uses your own spirit as a light to illuminate what's within you, Proverbs 20:27.** All dreams need interpretation.

God perfectly prepared Jacob mentally through the spirit dream to accept his destiny. A spirit dream is not an ordinary dream in which we process our thoughts and emotions, it's an insertion from God. As a result, it brought a perception change to accept fixed events set in motion that defied natural things. After seeing God and angels in his dream in the wilderness, "Jacob awoke from his sleep and said, "Surely the Lord is in this place, and I did not know it." There's a change in Jacob and he now does not see a desolate place, he's aware that he's encountering God and being led.

"I will praise the Lord, who counsels me; even at night my heart instructs me. I keep my eyes always on the Lord. With him at my right hand, I will not be shaken." Psalm 16:7-8.

Some types of dreams.

- Processing the day - This is us 'sleeping on it' just as we'd do with a problem that we're looking to solve. This helps us function better.

- Lucid Dreams - You are aware you are dreaming and may have control over your dream and will remember parts or all of the dream. Messages from our minds or from God can be contained in these and can be very revealing about ourselves and our lives.

- Prophetic Dreams - They show aspects of something future, like a warning or an event that's about to happen or a solution to a current issue in your life. These dreams can also open up possibilities you never even thought of, for example, a way for you to prosper. These dreams require action on your part, whether in doing or preparing for it.

- Nightmares - They cause distressing emotions during the dream. They can occur because you have watched or experienced something traumatic, or you have stress or anxiety about something or due to illness, emotional difficulties or you use certain medications, drugs or chemicals. In some cases, it may be the result of an invasive spiritual presence of a malevolent kind. Recurring nightmares may have a buried memory at their root, so, it's helpful to record these and pray about them.

- Impartation dreams - These dreams can be understood as a spiritual 'download' or 'upgrade' from God. You'll find clarity on spiritual aspects and things pertaining to you uniquely. This is an intimate encounter between you and God with a very specific purpose. Jeremiah 23:28; Daniel 2.

- Directive dreams - Dreams can be directive, pointing you in the direction you should go, the path you should follow or the decision you should make. They give knowledge and wisdom to all people. Here are a few examples:

-Increase – Genesis 31:10-13; Genesis 41:15-32; 1 Kings 3.

-Strategic dreaming – Judges 7:13-15.

-Warning – Genesis 20:3-7; Matthew 2:12-13; Matthew 27:19.

-Destiny – Genesis 37; Genesis 40.

Mind dream or Spirit dream?

It's not the content or elements of the dream that determine if it's a process of your mind or a spirit dream, it's the depth. Both serve different purposes and are important in their own ways. What is the difference between the two and why does it matter? Let me explain.

Spirit dreams have rich colour and are vibrant – like you're seeing more of the colour spectrum and seeing in a way you don't see with your ordinary sight. You feel like you're in another dimension, things feel tangible. There's a sense in you that this is more than an ordinary dream.

Mind dreams have a normal amount of colour or they're muted in colour, even monochrome and feel like they operate within your normal processes in this earthly dimension.

Both mind dreams and spirit dreams may contain bizarre symbols or happenings. Your mind dreams may be processing and making stories of difficult and contradicting life themes. In spirit dreams, these strange elements or happenings could contain symbolism or prophetic elements that need prayerful consideration and interpretation. **In both cases, God will lead you to the answer if you spend time with Him about the dreams.**

Write down as much of the dream as soon as you wake. Each symbol or element or aspect could be significant, so, like Daniel, write it down so that you may consider the full dream.

Think about what each part, symbol or content of the dream means to you as an individual. Ask yourself a question about why that means that and think about how it could apply in your current life. Pray and listen to God to understand how He is leading your through the dream.

Applying these simple recommendations to your routine will bring you great benefits and allow you to use the gift of dreaming to enhance your waking life and help clarify what God is saying through your dreams.

Prayer: "Thank You loving Father, for all the ways You lead me. I want to use every opportunity to hear You and respond. Holy Spirit, guide me in understanding my dreams.

Help me deal with those things you reveal and take action to flow in what You're leading me into."

This is my time

Joseph didn't know that Mary was still a virgin who'd miraculously conceived. So, he's on the brink of ending their engagement. Then God communicates with him:

-He dreamed a dream from God and received knowledge and leading, then a dream to warn them to leave, then a dream to tell them it was safe to return.

Likewise, your spirit dreams are a way for God to lead you. To become more receptive and gain the most from them, check through these statements about dreams:

-I accept that there are ordinary dreams and dreams from God. He's always led through dreams and He may use dreams to instruct, warn or transform me.

-I accept that in my ordinary dreams and God-given dreams, I can get to know myself better. I can do this by recording my dreams in a dream journal, talking about them and thinking about them.

-I treat my dreams as a valid tool to enhance my life and a way that God will lead me.

-I accept that God can use my dreams to speak to

me, direct me, reveal my destiny, give me insight, show me what's ahead, prosper me and warn me and so, I take note.

-I accept that dreams need interpretation.

-I accept that a spirit dream is not an ordinary dream in which we process our thoughts and emotions, it's an insertion from God.

-I accept that a spirit dream results in a perception change.

-I accept that spirit dreams often require action on my part, whether in doing or preparing.

How did you go?

Did you find you could agree with all the points?

Yes? Being receptive to spirit dreams is a blessing.

No? We're not taught to observe dreams, so some reservations are normal. Go over the chapter prayerfully asking God to open you to dreams and visions of the night.

-Can you recall dreams you've had that informed, warned or guided you?

-How were you led in the dreams?

-Did you keep a record?

-Did you act on what was shown?

Steps I will take

-Consider recording your dreams in a dream journal.

-Write down as much of the dream as soon as you wake. Details fade and are forgotten quickly.

-Think about what each part, symbol or content of the dream means to you as an individual. Ask yourself a question about why that means that and think about how it could apply in your current life.

-Pray and listen to God to understand how He is leading your through the dream.

-In spirit dreams, each symbol or element or aspect could be significant, so, like Daniel, write it down so that you may consider the full dream.

-God will lead you to the answer when you spend time with Him about the dreams.

Applying these simple recommendations will bring you great benefits, enhance your life and help clarify what God is saying through your dreams.

Coming up

God led Joseph into his life calling as the protector of the Saviour and Mary. So, once you have some idea of what you're becoming, how do you take what you know in your heart and mind and birth it into the world? Let's see how a young girl birthed a vision that changed the world…

BEING LED IN YOUR VISION WALK

"What is impossible with men is possible with God." Luke 18:27.

Excerpt adapted from the Thoughts on the Way article entitled 'Crab Baskets and Plans'

You've got it! You know some or all of what you should do with your life. Great! What now? How do you take the knowledge God has led you into and translate it in the real world? What do you do with the vision of your life you have? How do you walk it out in your life?

Let's take a REALLY hard example of a Vision Walk as our object lesson: **a virgin with a vision.**

You can read how it starts in Luke 1:26-38. Triumphantly, Mary took the revelation and the promise from God that the angel Gabriel offered her, believed and through her consent opened the way for the Messiah by declaring "…Behold, the maidservant of the Lord! Let it be to me according to your word…"

We often stop there without pondering the nine months that followed after that history changing moment.

In whom could she confide that God had parted eternity and entered her womb? Who'd believe her? What of the law? No doubt, that young maiden had much to think about and even more to dread from those strict, law-abiding, religious folk who surrounded her. What was she to do with this growing revelation and promise in the face of isolation or death?

We discover what Mary wisely chose to do in Luke 1:39-40: "(She)... arose in those days and went into the hill country **with haste**, to a city of Judah and entered the house of Zacharias and greeted Elizabeth..."

You'll never be alone as you journey. God will be your travelling companion on your Vision Walk. God gave the vision, and He will lead. Expect it and notice His leading.

God had let Mary know that Elizabeth was pregnant. And she took note. He'd pointed her in the direction to go. So, take time to carefully consider what the vision is showing you and everything God tells you about it. Ask God for clarity and His leading.

Mary hurried away from those who could not understand and who could harm her. And hurried toward the one person she knew who'd understand what was happening.

When God's messenger, Gabriel proclaimed God's announcement to Mary, he'd also given her strategic information: "(Elizabeth)... your relative has also conceived a son in her old age; and this is now the sixth month for her who was called barren." Luke 1:36. It showed her the path to take on her Vision Walk - and that path led to support.

On your Vision Walk journey, as you're walking out the promise and the revelation, you'll always be accompanied - God will be with you. And He will provide someone or a cluster of supporters who will share the walk with you.

Elizabeth and Mary shared a common experience that created a bond - the announcement by God's messenger Gabriel that they'll have God ordained conception. Elizabeth when she was past the age of conception and Mary through a unique miracle, as a virgin.

Mary and Elizabeth were both birthing a single, historical, eternity changing event. Although it's not recorded in the Bible, they must have spent much time in those three months encouraging each other and praying for each other.

Vision Walk expectation.

For Elizabeth, as her belly grew, her faith grew. She'd have the resilience to withstand those who had considered her cursed, or, at least, totally out of favour with God. Why, they'd even called her 'Barren.'

And even her husband, a servant of God, was less than expectant - until... Zechariah asked the angel,

"How can I be sure of this? I am an old man, and my wife is well along in years."

Well now, Zechariah has given us a lesson on how to offend an angel. Just tell him you don't believe God's message. In his heart he lacked trust in God. With no expectancy or vision his speech would have been faith-draining.

The birth of John, the forerunner to Jesus, was a fixed event in God's plans. It would happen. But without doubt, Zechariah would be spreading his doubt and unbelief by saying, "I can't believe..."

The remedy?

God prevents his faith destroying utterances. That messenger had authority to deal with this: He said to Zechariah, "I am Gabriel. I stand in the presence of God, and I have been sent to speak to you and to tell you this good news. And now you will be silent and not able to speak until the day this happens, because you did not believe my words, which will come true at their appointed time." See Luke 1:18-20.

What have we just seen? God dealing with a person who would have dragged Elizabeth down with his words. Within Elizabeth, the forerunner of the Messiah was being knitted by God into the voice that would make the paths straight for the coming King. His prophetic destiny already fixed in that tiny body he moved about in.

Mary arrives: "When Elizabeth heard Mary's

greeting the babe leaped in her womb, and Elizabeth was filled with the Holy Spirit... 'But why is it granted to me, that the mother of my Lord should come to me?... Blessed is she who believed, for there will be a fulfillment of those things which were told her from the Lord'" Luke 1:41-45.

Your Vision Walk of promise always has God's confirmation of His word through witnesses.

Gabriel the Messenger of God appeared to Zechariah and due to his unbelief, struck him mute as the first sign. The second is Mary's acceptance of the word of Gabriel and the overshadowing by the Holy Spirit. And next, John, the prophetic voice for Christ leaps in the womb of Elizabeth and she prophesies.

When your Vision Walk is done, others catch a glimpse of the promise and the revelation.

Both women faced opposition and had to nurture the vision as well as the child in them. Elizabeth's neighbours and relatives rejoiced with her - but when? At the birth of her son. Understand that those around you will not have the vision you have, so they will only realise your Vision Walk once it's been birthed.

A Pregnant Virgin returns.

Mary, a virgin, returns home with a swollen belly, pregnant with the vision of her destiny. She now faces those who haven't heard and don't know. Even just Joseph struggles with the reality that confronts him. He seeks a way to spare her even though he didn't understand. Joseph thought to "…put her away secretly" so she wouldn't have to face stoning. **God intervenes.** Matthew 1:20. **God's messenger explains why.** It's by the Holy Spirit that she's conceived. She will give birth to a Son who's to be named Jesus as He's the Saviour.

Joseph's response? He did what the messenger of God instructed him to do. See Matthew 1:19-25. God intervened in order to prepare Joseph to support Mary during her pregnancy, to help in the birth and as they made a loving home for the Child in their care.

On her Vision Walk, God was with Mary, step by step. He led her to Elizabeth to walk together. He then brought Joseph alongside her on the journey - a journey with Jesus.

Your Vision Walk.

Likewise, your Vision Walk begins as you take the first step by believing what God sets before you. Be strong - you'll face opposition and even doubters as you climb out of the ordinary and step into walking out the vision. **As you hold true on your Vision Walk, God will flesh out the promise and the revelation of the vision until you reach your destination.**

Prayer: "Show me how to build resilience and how to grow as a person as I Vision Walk. Thanks you for those who walk with me and for the evidence of Your constant leading and care at this time. Show me how I may be a blessing to those who are with me in this Vision Walk."

This is my time

We studied Mary's Vision Walk taking note of the lessons in it. Now, let's take what we found and set it out for our own Vision Walk as a check list.

-I have received a promise from God and believed it. I now know some or all of what I should do. I'm ready to walk out this vision in my life.

-I consider carefully who I can confide in. It has to be those who will believe, encourage and support me on this journey.

-I will be cautious about sharing with those who won't understand and who could undermine my expectations and efforts.

-I trust that I will not be alone on my journey. God will be my travelling companion on my Vision Walk. God gave the vision, and He will lead me. I expect it and take note of His leading.

-As I walk out the promise and the revelation, God will provide someone or a cluster of supporters who will share the walk with me.

-I take time to carefully consider what the vision is showing me and everything God tells me about it. I ask God for clarity and His leading.

-I act on what I'm shown. When Gabriel revealed that Mary's cousin Elizabeth was pregnant, she hastened to her. She'd been shown the path to take on her Vision Walk - and it led to support.

-Where possible, I will associate with others with a common experience to encourage each other and pray for each other.

-I will nurture the promise through believing thoughts and words. Zechariah asked "How can I be sure of this? I am an old man, and my wife is well along in years." He lacked trust in God. With no expectancy or vision his speech would have been faith-draining.

-I will avoid listening to people like Zechariah who spread doubt and unbelief.

-I will note further encouragements God gives me. In Mary's case, John the Baptist leapt in the womb of Elizabeth when Mary greeted her. Then Elizabeth was filled with the Holy Spirit and further confirmed Mary's Vision Walk through prophecy.

-My Vision Walk of promise will have God's confirmation of His word through witnesses.

-I understand that it's when my Vision Walk is done, that others will catch a glimpse of the promise and the revelation. They weren't given the vision I have, so they will only realise my Vision Walk once it's been birthed.

-Where necessary, God will communicate with those around me to support my Vision Walk just as He did with Joseph in a dream. He brought Joseph alongside Mary on the journey.

How did you go?

The Vision Walk principles you've just examined come straight from Mary's experience. Were you encouraged?

Yes? You're able to set out with confidence.

No? Take heart. You can do it. Take the lessons from this chapter and consider them prayerfully. And seek out positive, faith building companions who'll encourage you. Remember too that in the chapter entitled 'Clarity and Courage' Gideon started with doubts but became a mighty man of faith, step by step.

Steps I will take

-My Vision Walk begins as I take the first step by believing what God sets before me.

-I'll be strong as I step into walking out the vision.

-As I hold true on my Vision Walk, God will flesh out the promise and the revelation of the vision until I reach my destination.

Coming up

Mary responded to a pivotal moment in her life and in the history of the world. Next, let's journey alongside some very wise and learned travellers who prepared and came ready to meet their pivotal event...

LIFE'S PIVOTAL MOMENTS

"The mind of man plans his way, but the Lord directs his steps." Proverbs 16:9 NKJV.

We've all had those pivotal moments - the moment in your life when an event or realisation changed your life. Something happens in these pivotal moments that changes your thinking and your living and some part or all of your life is different.

Some experience their pivotal moment and are instantly changed, like Paul on the road to Damascus or Peter, James and John seeing Jesus transfigured in front of them. Paul had no idea when he set out for Damascus that his life would be changed on the road there. The three disciples with Jesus didn't know they'd climb the mountain as men and come down the mountain as apostles. We rarely see the lead up to a pivotal event, the 'stuff' that's happening to set the right conditions for that moment that will change us.

Sometimes, we have glimpses before the event that this will be life changing, like expecting a child. But you only experienced the full impact of that pivotal moment when you held your child for the first time and realized what that meant. I'm sure, as you read this, that you've thought of a pivotal moment in your own life and how that changed you.

We see the final moment of the pivotal event, the place where we are changed by what happens. Yet, many pivotal events have a lead up to them. **It's you moving towards something God planned, so you can reach a new level in your life. God, who knows the number of hairs on your head and each sparrow that falls is leading you to and through those pivotal events.**

One way this happens is when God 'inserts' some scenes and events in your life that will use your abilities to take you to the pivotal event. Let me explain by taking us back to a group of men from the east on a dark road following a star...

Balthasar rolled up the scroll and placed it beside the others in his saddle bag. He had meticulously recorded the long and arduous journey as they followed the star in growing wonder and anticipation. He and his companions knew the prophecy found in the words of Isaiah 60:1-6: "kings [coming] to the brightness of your dawn" bearing "gold and frankincense." Their gifts were fitting for the new-born king.

In Jerusalem they wondered that no-one else spoke of the new king. "For we observed his star at its rising, and have come to pay him homage." They met king Herod who questioned them long and deeply to find out when exactly the star appeared and he asked them to return and tell him when they find the child. After they'd heard the king, they set out; and there, ahead of them, went the star that they had seen at its rising, until it stopped over the place where the child was. When they saw that the star had stopped, they were overwhelmed with joy. Finally, they were here!

The account given in the Gospel of Matthew doesn't state that they were present on the night of the birth; in the Gospel of Luke, Joseph and Mary remain in Bethlehem until it is time for Jesus' dedication, in Jerusalem, and then return to their home in Nazareth. Matthew 2:1-12 takes up our story of their visit to Jesus in a house (not a stable), with only his mother mentioned as present. "On entering the house, they saw the child with Mary his mother; and they knelt down and paid him homage. Then, opening their treasure chests, they presented to him their gifts of gold, frankincense, and myrrh."

The gifts reveal their knowledge.

All three gifts are offerings and gifts given to a king. Myrrh being commonly used as an anointing oil, frankincense as a perfume, and gold as a valuable. The three gifts had a spiritual meaning: gold as a symbol of kingship on earth, frankincense (an incense) as a symbol of deity, and myrrh (an embalming oil) as a symbol of death.

These learned wise men were versed in knowledge and were wise – they understood the significance of what they were part of. They had left their countries and travelled for many months at expense to themselves to come to fulfil their part of the prophecy.

They knew and understood the pivotal event that was unfolding by the gifts they gave. And it's only in the moment of being face to face with this pivotal event that the full impact of the moment is understood – the moment they are face to face with the King of all the world.

Leading beyond the event.

Whether your pivotal event happened suddenly as it did to Paul on the Damascus road or you had some foreknowledge like the wise men, the pivotal moment will change you. You've had this pivotal moment and you have to take what has happened and do something with it. You have to decide to allow the change that happened through God's leading to this pivotal event to 'stick.'

We see this clearly in the record of Paul's life and we can draw out a pattern of what we can do too. Let's take a look.

Paul gets the shock of his life on the road to Damascus. He finds that he'd been a zealous enemy of God. What to do? That's the burning question. Should he return to his profession as a tentmaker? What is he to do?

Paul does the only wise thing – he seeks God in prayer and fasts to hear Him more clearly. In response, he's given a vision that a certain Ananias is on his way to him. While Ananias discussed going to Paul, with the Lord, this is what he's told…

"Go, for he is a chosen vessel of Mine to bear My name before Gentiles, kings, and the children of Israel... I will show him how many things he must suffer for My name's sake." Acts 9:15-16.

Paul has already received a vision from God, heard the name Ananias and knows that this man will pray for him to regain his sight. And as we read, he's yet to receive more instructions about his future. "I will show him... "

As we know, Paul was a man attentive in prayer to God's leading and instructions. And he was a man of action who did what he knew to do. After ending his fast, and recovering his strength he joins with other believers to apply his abilities...

"Immediately he preached the Christ in the synagogues, that He is the Son of God." And he kept growing in his calling. See Acts 9:10-22.

Paul urged believers to copy him as he copied the Lord. **Seeking God in prayer follows our pivotal experience because God will be speaking to us about His plans.** We then live out what we're instructed to do and start with what we knew, growing step by step in our service to God.

Prayer: "Help me to recognise pivotal events in my life whether they are sudden or come with some foreknowledge. Show me how to take what happened and do what You want with it."

This is my time

A pivotal moment is a moment in your life when an event or realisation changed your life.

-Can you identify any pivotal moments that you've had that happened suddenly to change your life?

-Can you identify any pivotal moments you've experienced in which you had some awareness in advance that you were being guided towards something God planned as a new level for you?

In Paul's Damascus road encounter he finds that he'd been a zealous enemy of God. What to do now? That's the burning question. Should he return to his profession as a tentmaker? What is he to do? We see his actions and God's leading beyond that pivotal moment.

-Examining Acts 9:10-22, what were the things Paul did to discover God's plans for him?

-What types of communication did God use to instruct Paul?

-Paul was a man attentive in prayer to God's leading and instructions. And he was a man of action who did what he knew to do. What actions did he take based on what he now knew?

How did you go?

Could you identify pivotal moments in your life?

Yes? You have an excellent opportunity to review how you responded and followed through.

No? Not a problem. Use your experience of coming into the kingdom as reference. That was a pivotal moment. Was it sudden? Did you notice progressive steps?

Steps I will take

-Think about your pivotal moments in the light of Acts 9:10-22. You can also find valuable pointers in the chapter entitled 'A close encounter'. How might you follow through on your next one based on what you studied?

-As we live out what we're instructed to do and start with what we know, we'll grow step by step. The result is amazing fulfilment in our life.

Coming up

Next, we'll look at how to flow in God's leading in those times in life we're faced with sorrow and death, those pivotal events of loss or hurt...

IN SORROW AND DEATH...

"As a mother comforts her child, so will I comfort you." Isaiah 66:13.

Excerpt from 'Tales out of Africa: Ordinary People having Extraordinary Encounters with God'
https://www.amazon.co.uk/dp/B0957GZKMP

It's a cool, overcast morning as my partner prepares a huge pot of homemade baked beans from scratch, eggs and sausages. Guests arrive for breakfast and drive the short distance down to my mom's house to pick her up. They reach her front door. It's unlocked. Strange. We'd asked her never to leave it open for safety. But this time, she must have left it open without knowing why.

They return without her. The look in their eyes tells me immediately that something is wrong. "Where's my mom?" Sorrowfully, they share that my mom's died. As always, in a crisis, I become totally calm, even though I'm devastated. I don't remember eating but I did, I need strength for what's ahead.

We go through to her home. It's a sweet, little house we'd recently bought just for her and we were in the process of renovating. She loved her little home because as a single mother raising three children, she'd never been able to own her own property. It was always a happy place filled with her love and we loved visiting. Not today. We enter. We walk through the silence to her bedroom.

I've steeled myself for what I'm about to see. The first thing I notice is the expression in her eyes. They're wide and happy as if she's surprised by who she's seeing. She's lying prostrate on her bed, dressed, ready for church, in a smart, black, two-piece, white blouse and modest gold jewellery. Her bible and her tithes and offerings envelope are next to her. Her head is tilted back, as she exhaled her last breath. She's so still. All life and animation have departed. All that's left is a motionless likeness as if a sculptor has rendered her perfectly in clay.

Thoughts and emotions swirl through me. We spoke on the phone the night before and arranged to see her first thing in the morning for church and to spend the day together. And that morning, looking at her lifeless body, I was in turmoil. For over a week I'd kept thinking that she was going to die but I rejected the thought. I did not know God was preparing me, leading me to accept it was her time and she was ready.

Over a dinner with us, the week before, in her favourite restaurant, she sat with a huge smile on her face. When I asked what she was smiling about she told me that she'd realised that she'd done everything she wanted to do in her life - from travelling to owning her own house.

As I stood and looked at her, I knew for sure that this morning, the loving Creator had come for her, in a personal way, in her home, when she was immaculately dressed, tithes by her side and ready. She must have sensed what was about to happen, which was why her door was unlocked, giving us access.

Into the stillness.

I couldn't measure my grief and my heart couldn't contain it. So, how do you get over pain so big you cannot fathom it? Enveloped in my grief and loss and constantly crying, I wandered around the house in exhaustion. The sense of loss was totally overwhelming. It felt so big, I couldn't even measure my pain. So, I did the only thing I knew would help me. I prayed.

I feel the presence of God settling on me and washing away my grief and pain to the point that I could stop crying and feel normal again. Some leading of God happens in the deep places of your soul, where only you and God experience it. I felt this leading now. As I felt the tug of God, I waited for God to lead and guide me through this.

I was standing in the kitchen in front of the sink and the next moment, I had an open vision. I see my mother standing on a sea of glass with her hands raised, head upward and her eyes closed. There's a brilliant light all around her. All the beauty of my mother's inner self is now fully manifested. She is revealed as her true spiritual self - timeless, straight-backed and magnificent. She's radiant, serene, beautiful and enraptured in worship. Peace and joy radiate out of her and power flows around her. And she's smiling happily. Relief flooded me. She was safe! Seeing my mom brought me peace and joy and started my healing.

This open vision was so powerful and so clear that, as I write, I'm transported right back to that moment in time when I saw my mom in all her splendour. It remains my secret comfort when I miss her now. Through the kindness of God, He led me in a vision to see beyond death and witness the glorious transformation of my beloved mom. To this day, I know, with certainty, that my mom is safe, forever, in a perfected state, with a loving God.

The grief is there, but so is God.

God experienced grief when Jesus "bore our griefs and carried our sorrows…" Isaiah 53:4. In our times of grief, sorrow and loss we have the sure presence of God with us. Just as God led Jesus through His darkest hour, He leads us. **In the midst of that deep pain is the sweetness of God's presence. It's also a place where God reveals what you need to take you forward.** With me it was seeing my mom safe and beautiful worshipping on the sea of glass.

Isaiah, in sorrow at the loss of his kinsman and earthly king, encountered his heavenly King. Standing outside the temple he saw "the Lord sitting on a throne, high and lifted up, and the train of His robe filled the temple." **In sorrow and loss and grief, God is there quietly leading us to experience His presence in the midst of our grief. It's not denying the pain or hiding from it but finding the leading of God in it.** He will meet you in a very special way and lead you through in the particular way you need in that moment. Although the leading of God is different and unique in every case, you are assured of the enveloping love of God in the midst of it.

Allowing yourself sorrow.

Many believers when facing the death of a loved one will say something like, 'I rejoice they're safe in heaven.' **Rejoicing in this knowledge is a great comfort BUT it will not bring you the healing you need. Grief at loss is a normal, healthy response.** When God showed me my mom safe and beautiful, it started the healing process. I still feel the loss and I still miss my mom all these many years later.

Each person of significance in our lives fills a 'space' in our lives – they occupy and fill in part of the very flow of our lives. When we lose someone, the space they filled in our lives is suddenly empty. That's a reality we face and we learn to live with that empty space that used to be filled with the life and person of the departed loved one. And that's hard.

I've done things along the way to honour and celebrate her life and in remembrance of her but I've not allowed myself to stay stuck in my loss. It's learning to carry that loss, knowing I can't fix it or make it go away. **The loss is there and it strengthened my belief to be present in my life and love the ones I have with me.**

In prayer, I regularly ask God to help me to be present and how to best live out my life and appreciate the people I know. And He has been there leading in each situation. He speaks and guides in unique ways for every situation and His deep love and comfort wraps around you and holds you tight in those hard and dark times when it seems there's no end to the sorrow or loss.

Like you, I've had times of sorrow and death in my life.

These are the things that helped me move through:

- Look yourself in the mirror and tell yourself, 'It's okay to feel sad, or tired (or whatever) at this moment. I'm working through something that doesn't make sense to me.

- Much of the work in early grief is done in your heart and mind, not outward actions. That's why you may forget to eat, or sleep or do other important or normal things. Set up a sticky note or prompt on your phone to remind you to eat or to do some of the other things you need to do in order to stay healthy.

- Feeling brain fog, that state of almost awake sleep cycle, is your mind going off-line so it can heal. It might not seem like much but tending to your physical needs, eating, sleeping, drinking water and moving your body as you're able, is one of the best ways to move out of this fog. Just moving about will allow your right brain to kick in and give you some light in the fog you're feeling.

- Even if you don't feel like it, get outside – feel the sun and remember nature won't care if you sit or cry, it's healing and soothing properties will still work on you even if you're not aware of it.

- Find something you can do like bathing your dog or picking some flowers and arranging them. It helps you connect to the present which will help your brain come out of neutral.

- When you're working through grief and loss you won't be as productive, so be gentle with yourself. Don't compare what you used to do with what you're doing now. Right now, you're not the same person, so give yourself the space to recover and become whole again.

- Say. "No thank you." to the well-meaning things others do that exhaust you or tax you emotionally. Gently tell them at this moment you can't handle that. At the same time, allow some new things in your life that could nourish you and participate – even if it's just for short periods of time.

- Above all else, stay connected to God, wrapped in His love. Pour your heart out to Him, cry, listen. This is where you will find the road that will lead you through the sorrow and on in your life. This is where you will find new meaning for your life.

"Even if I walk through the valley of the shadow of death... You are with me; Your rod and Your staff, they comfort me." Psalm 23.

Prayer: "Dear Spirit, I know you are with me as my Comforter and Guide. I am in sorrow and pain; I find it hard to just be and to do the things of life. I need your strength today so I can take a step forward. Lead me, comfort me and guide me and help me find meaning even in the midst of my pain."

This is my time

In this chapter, 'In sorrow and death', I shared my very personal experience with the loss of a loved one, my mother. Here I've set out God's leading to help in coping and healing.

-Receiving news of a loved one's death is distressing. Be gentle with yourself as you come to terms with your loss.

-To help me cope with the overwhelming grief and loss. I did the only thing I knew would help me. I prayed.

-One of the benefits I received from praying was that I

felt the presence of God settling on me and washing away my grief and pain to the point that I could stop crying and feel normal again.

-Some leading of God happens in the deep places of your soul, where only you and God experience it. I felt this leading. As I felt the tug of God, I waited for God to lead and guide me through this.

-I prayed for assurance that my mom was safe with Him. And God gave me a vision to see beyond death and witness my mom's glorious transformation. Seeing my mom brought me peace and joy and started my healing.

-The grief is there, but so is God. We have the sure presence of God with us. He leads us. In the midst of that deep pain is the sweetness of God's presence.

-In His presence we're shown what we need to take us forward. With me it was seeing my mom safe and beautiful worshipping.

-We don't deny the pain or hide from it but we find the leading of God in it. He will meet you in a very special way and lead you through in the particular way you need in that moment.

-The leading of God is different and unique in every case. You are assured of the enveloping love of God in the midst of it.

-Stay connected to God, wrapped in His love. Pour your heart out to Him, cry, listen.

Steps I might take

If you're going through loss now, you're in pain, use this chapter to help you heal.

-Re-reading the section entitled 'These are the things that helped me move through' can assist you too.

-Stay connected to God, wrapped in His love. Pour your heart out to Him, cry, listen.

-Give yourself time.

Coming up

When you're ready to start healing, in the next chapter, we'll meet a man with leprosy who gets a 'water healing'...

LEADING IN HEALTH AND HEALING

"(Naaman) went down and dipped seven times in the Jordan, according to the saying of the man of God; and his flesh was restored." 2 Kings 5:14.

Excerpts from 'Tales out of Africa: Ordinary People having Extraordinary Encounters with God'
https://www.amazon.co.uk/dp/B0957GZKMP and
'The Fruit of the Spirit: the way to whole and happy living.'
https://www.amazon.co.uk/dp/B08MYXVDQ6

One of the greatest adventures in God leading is how He leads you in living in health and healing. We've had amazing experiences in both and have learnt that God treats each healing as unique. A one-off event. This is certainly the case with our next story that, to my knowledge, has never been exactly repeated.

"Now Naaman, commander of the army of the king of Syria, was a great and honourable man in the eyes of his master, because by him the Lord had given victory to Syria. He was also a mighty man of valour, but a leper." An incurable and horrible disease worked in the body of this man with no relief or cure in sight.

On one of their raids, they captured a young girl from Israel who ended up waiting on Naaman's wife. Through this girl they learn that there is a prophet who can heal Naaman and without delay the king sends him with an extravagant gift to the king of Israel. The king sees it as a ploy to stir up trouble between the kingdoms. Elisha hears about it and sends a message, "Please let him come to me, and he shall know that there is a prophet in Israel."

Elisha gives a very specific instruction to Naaman: "Go and wash in the Jordan seven times, and your flesh shall be restored to you, and you shall be clean." Now the problem with very specific instructions is that we may not always understand them or see the sense of them. This was the case with Naaman. He wanted pomp, honour and ceremony. This is what he expected: "But Naaman became furious, and went away and said, "Indeed, I said to myself, 'He will surely come out to me, and stand and call on the name of the Lord his God, and wave his hand over the place, and heal the leprosy." Pre-conceived ideas of how we should be healed can get in the way of us doing what God actually tells us to do, just as it did for Naaman.

His servants convince him to follow the prophet's words and after dipping seven times in the Jordan, "his flesh was restored like the flesh of a little child, and he was clean." God went beyond healing him, God made him whole and through this Naaman becomes a worshipper of God! 2 Kings 5:17-18.

A tale of two burns.

We shared this story in 'Tales out of Africa: Ordinary People having Extraordinary Encounters with God.' It really illustrates how God will lead completely differently to bring healing to the same injury.

"Uh!" I jerked my hand out of the oven. The intense heat had scorched the skin right off the top of my hand. Excruciating! The sickly-sweet smell of charred skin rising into my nostrils added to my trauma. My partner rushed into the kitchen. I held out my arm, palm down. The back of my hand was red, raw, raging in pain. The top and lower levels of skin were gone and the edges were shrivelled and browned. I tried to nurse my hand by placing it under cold, running water but the intense throbbing raged on. I was in shock and the hospital was too many miles away to treat this rapidly.

I needed prayer right there and then. As my hand was far too painful for contact, I placed my left hand slightly above it and my partner's hand hovered below it. We prayed. Then, I moved my hand away and stared - my hand was healed. I don't mean that I believed it was healed or it felt healed or even that the swelling had begun to subside, no, this was instantaneous and miraculous! Where the top and lower layers of the skin were gone, there was now perfect skin. The pain was gone. Even though the damage had been so very bad there wasn't a sign that my hand had ever been burnt - no mark, no scar. We were astonished and overjoyed.

About 7 years later, I was going to have another serious burn. This time, it was going to be treated by the Spirit in a very odd way – at least, odd to us.

I'd touched a hot surface and as I pulled my hand away, I saw how badly burnt my hand was. There was a blistered, raw patch about an inch in circumference where the skin had been seared. The Spirit instructed me, "Put raw cabbage leaves on the burn with camomile (chamomile) lotion." My hand was too badly burnt for me to prepare it, so my partner made the mix and applied the poultice. The redness and heat left and within a few days, the scar was healed leaving no marks. Once again, even though the burn had been very bad there was no sign that the skin had ever been damaged.

Years later, I'm watching a programme on television. It's about life in the Philippines. Tucked into this cultural documentary was a segment on a traditional treatment for burns - a poultice of cabbage leaf and camomile. I just smiled and nodded.

We decided to investigate the medicinal use of cabbage leaf and camomile along with their therapeutic properties. Yes, cabbage leaf had long been used in folk remedies for burns in many countries. It's anti-inflammatory, reduces swelling and it's cooling. And camomile? Its medicinal use can be traced to ancient times for many ailments. Applied to burns, it's antispasmodic, anti-inflammatory, pain-relieving, germicidal but use with care if you're allergic to daisies or ragweed. Combining cabbage leaves and camomile? Although the television program showed it being used in the Philippines, search as we would, there were no other references to combining them. How very odd. You'd think there must be something, wouldn't you? Nothing. We'd gently been given a profound lesson - those who trust in the Spirit have access to vast knowledge. It's far beyond what's understood, commonly available and far beyond our limited intellect.

God never ceases to amaze us. Here was the same emergency, severe skin burn, healed in two very different ways. Why had God surprised us with a mind-boggling instant, regenerative healing in one case and a medical treatment with progressive healing in the other? Puzzling. Over the years, we've prayed about pain, injury or sickness with many different results. Sometimes instantaneous restoration. Sometimes progressive recovery. Sometimes, we had to keep on keeping on praying. Sometimes the Spirit gave specific instructions."

Being open to the Spirit's leading in health.

As you saw in the story you've just read, God healed the same medical condition in two ways, the first was a miraculous instant healing the second was progressive using a medicinally sound treatment. In both cases, a complete healing resulted. At the time, we were puzzled. Now we understand - the Spirit was training us to be more and more responsive to His leading in health and healing and every aspect of life.

And this brings us to a very important point. We often follow formulas we've learnt from other believers. Life in the Spirit is far beyond formulas as this pastor with a healing ministry was to discover – while having a shower...

Ray was a respected pastor with a notable healing ministry. He was a man of faith who prayed for the sick through the laying on of hands (Mark 16:18). He also sent out anointed cloths imbued with God's power through prayer and touch like Paul did (Acts 19:12). And he operated in the gifts of healings (1 Corinthians 12:28) that work to release a specific area or areas of healing such as praying for bone issues, eye issues and so on. Ray had been thoroughly trained through a bible-based ministry that understood healing and faith. He applied what he'd learnt and had seen with dedication. People came from all over to have him lay hands and pray for their healing.

But Ray had agonising joint pain that was getting worryingly worse and worse. He believed God for healing, he had the most effective prayers in his church pray over him, he was anointed with oil (James 5:14). And his pain kept growing. It was becoming so serious that it was affecting his movement. He kept asking God why he wasn't healed. He was doing everything he knew to do.

Ray's taking a shower, relaxing in the pleasant, hot flow of steamy water when the Spirit speaks to answer his question: "You're eating too much red meat. Cut down how much steak you eat and how often." Ray loved devouring big, juicy steaks every day and wrongly believed that the more red meat he ate the more he could build his muscles. He heard the Spirit's leading, adjusted his diet and was healed of joint pain within weeks.

Of course, if you have joint pain, it might be something completely different so, pray, seek God and ensure you see your doctor.

Healing of the whole person through many means.

Over the years, we've applied our knowledge of biblical healing and health. It's a vast subject. And we've always sought to be open to the Spirit's leading as He knows far more than we do and what method He wants to use.

As we've seen, healing includes prayer. It also includes much more. In all this is the leading of the Spirit. Should you pray about pain, injury or sickness once as we've done or persist in ongoing praying as we've done? The Spirit knows. Should you bathe in a river, a pool stirred by an angel, lay hands? He knows. What steps must I take in regard to diet, supplements, environment, stress and work? He knows that too. The Spirit often gives specific instructions like using cabbage and camomile to heal a burn, reducing red meat consumption in Ray's case. Paul had a powerful healing ministry, he also travelled with Luke, a practising, much loved doctor (Colossians 4:14) and advised his trainee to take a little wine for his various ailments (1 Timothy 5:23). Jesus told a family to feed their daughter after he raised her from the dead Mark 5:43.

What does all this tell us? Pray for healing and health, do what you know, seek medical advice, and stay ever open to God's leading.

Healing of mind.

Healing is a broad subject. And it extends beyond healing of the physical body it includes healing of our mind and our whole being. That old saying, healthy mind, healthy body does contain truth. So many physical conditions stem from distress, sorrow and other out of balance thoughts and emotions. As an example, "A merry heart does good, like medicine, but a broken spirit dries the bones." Proverbs 17:22.

God wants to heal our minds and give us a sound mind. It's right there in Jesus' mandate: "The Spirit of the LORD is upon Me... He has anointed Me To preach the gospel... heal the broken-hearted, proclaim liberty to the captives... recovery of sight to the blind... set at liberty those who are oppressed." Luke 4:18. Our mental wellbeing is so important to God that it's right after Jesus sharing the Good News in His mandate!

Just as in physical healing, our mental and spiritual healing involves doing the things we know to do and being led by the Spirit. Every believer works on mental cleaning, conforming their thinking to God's perfect ways, bringing thoughts and emotions under the influence of the Spirit and it all leads to a sound mind.

Holding on to emotions like regret, anger, jealousy and the like actually create effects in your physical body. The bible states that you create your life out of your heart. Proverbs 4:23.

The Fruit of the Spirit was given as healing to the damage the marring effect that wrong thinking has on our mental realm: our emotions, our will, our intellect, our imagination and our memory and the way the damage in the mental realm changes our perception and the way we respond to God, life and others. In order to reign in this life and the next effectively, we need to embrace the healing offered and co-operate with the Spirit as He leads to make this healing happen. To learn more about this, we recommend 'The Fruit of the Spirit: the way to whole and happy living.' https://www.amazon.co.uk/dp/B08MYXVDQ6

2 Timothy 1:7 "For God has not given us a spirit of fear, but of power and of love and of a sound mind." A 'safe mind' is what sound mind means in this verse. You have safe thinking that's revealed in good and wise judgment, disciplined and fruit producing thought patterns and the ability to understand right and to make right and fruitful decisions that enlarge your life and prosper you. We co-operate with God's leading to

make this happen by creating our new minds – putting off the old and putting on the new.

So, follow God's leading and explore and delight in your inner world and the mental and emotional abilities you have and find ways to maximize them by lovingly growing your mind and self.

You're led to live in wholeness and health.

As we grow more sensitive and responsive to the leading of God we will be taken far beyond our limited knowledge in our health, our healing and every aspect of our life. We can live a life of ongoing adventures in God's continual leading.

"And the Lord will guide you continually and satisfy your desire in scorched places and make your bones strong; and you shall be like a watered garden, like a spring of water, whose waters do not fail." Isaiah 58:11.

Prayer: "Lead me in how to enjoy health and healing for myself and to help others. I will seek to follow all your instructions and stay open to solutions beyond my understanding."

This is my time

God wants you to live in health and healing. With this in mind, check through these key principles to help you optimise wellness.

-I accept that God treats each healing as unique. And so, I stay alert to His leading like in the case of the two burns – one healed by prayer instantly, the other by treatment over time.

-I understand that, at times, God uses unexpected procedures such as with Naaman dipping in the Jordan seven times to be cured of leprosy. There's no natural explanation why this worked to heal him.

-I accept that I may not always understand the instruction or see the sense of it. This was the case in the instruction to apply cabbage and camomile to a burn which turned out to have medical benefits in treating burns.

-I accept that God may lead me in many different ways in praying about pain, injury or sickness. I may see instantaneous restoration, progressive recovery, I may need to keep on praying.

-I am open to the Spirit's leading in health and healing.

-When I don't find healing, I can ask God why in order to find out from God if there is a factor such as diet imbalance.

-I accept that to be effective in praying for sick people I need to be thoroughly trained through a bible-based ministry that understands healing and faith.

-I accept that I should pray, seek God and ensure I see a doctor.

-I understand that the Spirit often gives specific instructions like using cabbage and camomile to heal a burn, reducing red meat consumption, steps to take in regard to diet, supplements, environment, stress.

-I know from the bible that a Christian doctor practised medicine (Colossians 4:14) that Paul told Timothy to take a little wine for his various ailments (1 Timothy 5:23). Therefore, medical aid is an accepted part of healing.

-I understand that healing includes mind and emotions. The Spirit brings healing to my whole being.

-I accept that I can pray for healing and health, do what I know, seek medical advice, and stay ever open to God's leading.

How did you go?

Were you able to accept all the principles set out above.

Yes? That's wonderful. Continue to allow God to guide you into health and wellbeing.

No? Healing is a complex subject with many outlooks. Take time to go over the chapter again prayerfully.

Steps I will take

-We recommend learning from experienced, mature bible-based believers who practise praying for the sick. As we spend time with others who are sensitive to God's leading it helps us rise to higher levels.

Coming up

The promise Jesus made in John 10:10 states He came to give us life, and life more abundantly - that means prospering in all areas of your life. Let's see how God leads us in our prospering...

HE LEADS TO PROSPER YOUR LIFE

"Thus says the Lord, your Redeemer, the Holy One of Israel: "I am the Lord your God, Who teaches you to profit, Who leads you by the way you should go." Isaiah 48:17.

Interesting thing about this scripture is that the root word for profit means 'to ascend' – going up to a new level. So, God teaches you in order to raise you up, elevate you in value. In other words, God teaches you how to climb higher to benefit your life. Clearly, this is way more than just having increased profit in a financial sense - more money, more investments, more assets. This is being raised up, benefiting, succeeding in every possible way, in all aspects of your life with God as your personal adviser.

We can see this wider understanding of God profiting you in the International Standard Version of the bible: "This is what the Lord says, your Redeemer, the Holy One of Israel: "I am the Lord your God, who teaches you how to succeed, who directs you in the path by which you should go." Isaiah 48:17.

Hold onto that concept of success and rising to new levels in your whole life. And to it God adds that He leads you by the way you should go. God teaches and leads you so you'll ascend, benefit, succeed!

It's an amazing promise, one that God puts His name to. He's making sure you know who's promising; the Lord, your Redeemer, The Holy One of Israel, I am the Lord your God. In one sentence, God tells you four times who's making that promise to you!

When you put your name to a promise your reputation is at stake. God declares His name four times, and has it recorded on Isaiah's scroll, so, He really wants you to take note of how seriously He takes His promise of leading you to prosper in all ways.

And He prospers with great abundance. Tucked into Paul's blessing in his letter to the fellowship in Ephesus is this extraordinary statement: "(God)... is able to do exceedingly abundantly above all that we ask or think, according to the power that works in us." Ephesians 3:20.

Exceedingly, abundantly more than anything you can ask God for or expect from Him. Add this to our understanding that God wants you to prosper in every way and we have an astonishing promise from God to us.

To help us fix this in our minds and hearts let's take a look at the abundant thinking of God.

Take stars. In the creation record we're told, rather incidentally, "He made the stars also." Genesis 1:16. In fact, He made all of the estimated 200 billion trillion stars in the universe.

And look around you at nature. There's abundance everywhere – the trees bear fruit, the flowers bloom, all of nature is geared to abundance because it reflects its creator. God is an abundant God.

God loves to produce growth and increase. Take a grain of wheat. Plant it and it will produce over 100 kernels. Then plant those and you have 10,000 seeds. Do it just four more times and you have, wait for it... 1,000,000,000,000 grains of wheat!

So, when God tells us pretty emphatically that He'll teach us to prosper in every way, exceedingly abundantly more than we can image? What an awe-inspiring gift!

The possibilities for you to prosper in your life are endless and that's why God added "I will lead you..." And we're not led blindly, but intelligently. God likes us finding out things He put in us. Like a big Easter egg hunt in the garden, He wants us to look around expectantly and discover all the gifts He placed there and then use them, enjoy them, and have fun with them. God likes it when you take what He's given you and you grow it in your life.

"Every good gift and every perfect (complete) gift (or endowment) is from above, coming down from the Father of lights with whom there is no variation or shadow due to change." James 1:17. God's gifts are complete and He gives them as an endowment: gifts, talents, abilities, mental wiring placed in us to enable us to use these endowed gifts to enlarge our lives.

God attaches your whole life and level of living to His leading and teaching.

This leading and teaching to prosper is vastly superior to mere intellectual knowledge and appraisal. As an example, a real-estate expert may know the market in depth. They may make a very authoritative calculation on property price trends. They can predict to some degree how supply and demand will affect prices – only God knows everything about the property market and its future perfectly. And that's why the leading of God gives you such an advantage. And, as we saw before, this applies to every aspect of your life, finances, certainly, and in all ways.

Added to this teaching and leading of God to prosper you is the spiritual empowering to maximise your results. Right now, as a believer, alive to the Spirit of God, you live in touch with the flow of heaven's power. It's the Spirit who gives you the power to create an abundant life in all ways.

You are living within the Spirit at this moment according to Acts 17:28. You're highly conscious of the physical dimension you live in, we all are. When we were born again by the Spirit of God, we started to become more and more aware of God and His communications to us – His teaching us and leading us. It helps to understand that you are a multi-dimensional being - you are a spirit with a mind that lives in a body. You function and live your life in all three places at the same time. And all three need to be in harmony. Can we see this in action?

Let's take an inventor working on a serious problem. Poultry waste. Millions and millions of tons of organic material that decays so slowly that it keeps on piling up. The inventor has studied, researched, experimented. No solution. And then, in response to prayer, the inventor is shown something they'd never considered and how it will work. They have to work physically and stay mentally buoyant until finally, they produce the right combination of steps to dissolve the waste into a valuable by-product. The result is due to a harmony of their spirit, mind and body. In order to understand how God leads you to prosper, you need to approach life as a whole being.

Let's take an expert in real-estate, who know God. They know their market and keep adding to their understanding. As they pray and seek God through listening, they're taught how to progress in their profession. One day, God leads them to the worst property in the best suburb. No one's interested in it and it's dropped in price to rock bottom. God shows them its potential. They buy it, labour to renovate it and sell it at a profit.

God will reveal how to prosper by teaching you and leading you. You do your part by using your mind, your body and by staying attuned to God and empowered by Him.

Prayer: "Thank you for Your promise to teach

me to prosper abundantly in every way. I will seek to be sensitive to your instructions through prayer and listening. Teach me and lead every day."

This is my time

God teaches and leads you so that you'll ascend, benefit and succeed in all ways. And it's far more than anything you can ask God for or expect from Him.

-With this in mind, go through these key points to ensure you gain the full measure of God's blessings for your life:

-I accept that God leads intelligently and wants me to go and discover and enjoy all the gifts waiting for me and grow them in my life as I use them.

-I accept that God's leading and teaching to prosper is far superior to my own knowledge and appraisal. Therefore, I'm always open to His guidance.

-I agree with the following statement: 'Right now, as a believer, alive to the Spirit of God, I live in touch with the flow of heaven's power. It's the Spirit who gives me the power to create an abundant life in all ways.

-I understand that I am living within the Spirit at this moment according to Acts 17:28.

-When I was born again by the Spirit of God, I started to become more and more aware of God teaching and leading.

-I accept that I am a spirit with a mind that lives in a body.

-I accept that God will reveal how to prosper by teaching me and leading me. I then use my mind, and I act. By staying attuned to God and empowered by Him the result is success.

How did you go?

Did you find that you agreed with most or all of these statements? Then, you must be feeling uplifted and expectant. That's great!

What if you're not sure about something? That's alright too. The things of the Spirit can take time to enter our everyday lives. Remember, you're already applying so many things right now.

Steps I will take

-Re-read anything that you need to gain clarity in and as you read, ask God to give you increased understanding.

-Keep in mind that God wants you to understand how He teaches and leads you. So, be assured that He will always help you.

Coming up

We've seen that God prospers us abundantly, not just financially, but in all ways. What does that cover and how do we prosper in each case? Let's see...

THE FULLNESS OF GOD'S LEADING

**"And God is able to make all grace abound to you,
so that having all sufficiency in all things at all
times, you may abound in every good work."
2 Corinthians 9:8.**

God wants to lead us to bless us and prosper us abundantly in all ways. "I pray that you may prosper in all things and be in health, just as your soul prospers." 3 John 1:2. What does 'in all things' cover? Is anything excluded? The key is in the word prosper which involves raising you up in every way. So, by implication, that's everything that's good and nothing that harms you.

"Every good gift and every perfect gift is from above, and comes down from the Father of lights, with whom there is no variation or shadow of turning." James 1:17. God wants to lead you to everything good and guide you away from what's bad.

We see this presented in David's inspired song to God that identifies Him as a shepherd who leads. In the opening verse of Psalm 23 is this all-encompassing statement, "I shall lack nothing." And then David sets out that this is about everything good. God leads to good things, keeps you from bad things and leads to good ways of living. And tying in with the exceedingly abundantly blessing of Ephesians 3:20 David sings, "My cup overflows. Certainly, goodness and lovingkindness pursue me all the days of my life."

Over and over, throughout the bible we find the assurance of God leading, empowering, blessing, prospering and giving biblical peace which means 'nothing is missing or broken in your life'. He leads His people to overflow in prosperity so that we can be a blessing to others as well.

"And God is able to make all grace abound to you, so that having all sufficiency in all things at all times, you may abound in every good work." 2 Corinthians 9:8. Abundance through God in all things and always – can we define that?

Yes. All through the bible you find what prosperity is. See the words bless, blessed, blessing? Those things mentioned are all forms of prospering. You've read the stories of the faithful people of God? Then, you saw them being prospered, how and with what.

There's so much. To help us take in the scope, let's set biblical prosperity into the main categories:

- ✓ Spiritual Prosperity
- ✓ Mental Prosperity
- ✓ Physical Prosperity
- ✓ Relational Prosperity
- ✓ Accomplishment Prosperity
- ✓ Professional Prosperity
- ✓ Financial Prosperity

✓ Material Prosperity

God will lead you in all of these and more – no matter what it is, God will teach and guide you. Let's drill deeper into these categories of prospering:

Spiritual Prosperity.

You were born again - your spirit was reborn through the Spirit of God and you're alive spiritually. And you entered into a loving relationship with your Creator – you're rich spiritually! Spiritual prosperity flows from your closeness to God. God is Spirit, you are a spirit and you're now connected to God. We can experience an ever increasing spiritual prosperity as we seek to be close to God. That's easy because we know how much God loves us and we know that He does good things in our life.

As we speak to God and stay responsive to God, He leads us and counsels us and provides us with wisdom about everything in our life. You can talk to God about anything and ask Him for His help - and as your loving Father, He will.

Through your spiritual connection with your Creator you receive the guidance and empowering to make positive changes in your thoughts, actions and lifestyle. As a result, you grow healthier in mind, body, relationships - every aspect of your life.

The Spirit of God flows through you just as sap in a tree will flow into its branches and you begin to produce the Fruit of the Spirit - love, joy, peace, patience, kindness, goodness, faithfulness, gentleness, self-control. Galatians 5:22-23.

And over and above all these spiritual riches in your life God adds spiritual abilities – you can pray for the sick to recover and as the Spirit chooses, you receive special gifts that help you and others called the Gifts of the Spirit:

"... the manifestation of the Spirit is given to each one for the profit of all: for to one is given the word of wisdom through the Spirit, to another the word of knowledge through the same Spirit, to another faith by the same Spirit, to another gifts of healings by the same Spirit, to another the working of miracles, to another prophecy, to another discerning of spirits, to another different kinds of tongues, to another the interpretation of tongues. But one and the same Spirit works all these things, distributing to each one individually as He wills." See 1 Corinthians 12:1-11.

In all of the abundant spiritual blessings that God bestows on you we find His leading.

To learn more about the Fruit and the Gifts we recommend these two books:

GIFTS for DESTINY and LIFE
https://www.amazon.co.uk/dp/1838021000

The Fruit of the Spirit: The way to whole and happy living
https://www.amazon.co.uk/dp/B08MYXVDQ6

Mental Prosperity.

Flowing from your Spiritual prosperity comes transformation of your mind - your intellect, emotions and will and how you use them. Because you're in relationship with God, you perceive His leading and guidance – He will continually lead you to align your thinking to His through speaking to you, various communications and through directing you to particular biblical texts.

We're led to renew our minds: "And do not be conformed to this world [any longer with its superficial values and customs], but be transformed and progressively changed [as you mature spiritually] by the renewing of your mind [focusing on godly values and ethical attitudes], so that you may prove [for yourselves] what the will of God is, that which is good and acceptable and perfect [in His plan and purpose for you]." Romans 12:2 Amplified Bible.

This leading in renewing of our minds requires our effort: "… we are taking every thought and purpose captive to the obedience of Christ." 2 Corinthians 10:5 Amplified Bible.

As an example, as the Spirit highlights our old thought patterns of greed, selfishness and self-centredness we respond. Those thoughts start to fade and are replaced with the fresh thought patterns of consideration, generosity and benevolence. And we benefit in our mental and emotional state resulting in greater happiness, contentment and self-respect.

God's leading in our thinking includes correcting our misconceptions and increasing our expectancy. Take money – for many people just saying the word creates conflicting thoughts in them. God will lead us to a sound thinking on it so that we may prosper financially in good ways.

God fills our mind with truth, knowledge, understanding and leads us to use this wisely. Take the principle of sowing and reaping for example and how it applies to prospering. And He gives us answers where there were questions and spiritual insights to guide our way.

And through the healing power of the Spirit, healthy thinking and healthy nutrition our mind can grow in ability over the years.

Physical Prosperity.

What a great advantage we have when we have God's leading in our health and healing. Firstly, we're led to understand how the Spirit affects health and healing. God's power heals through our spiritual connection and intensifies through our faith. As we're led to understand about how God can heal us, we expect to receive healing through prayer, laying on of hands and all we see in the bible.

This leading is an extraordinary gift from God. When we add to it the leading of the Spirit then it gets even more extraordinary. He will lead as to whether you should pray about pain, injury or sickness once or persist in ongoing prayer. He may give leading in a particular procedure such as applying a poultice of cabbage and camomile to the burn as we read earlier.

God will lead us concerning factors that affect our health such as our diet, supplements, environment, unhealthy levels of stress. He may warn us, in advance, to stop doing something harmful such as smoking, or over-eating and shows us the consequence of neglecting to follow through on this leading. In the same way, He may show you that a mild symptom is far more serious than it appears and what to do about it.

He may lead us into a more balanced attitude to the medical services available to us. After all, Paul who had a powerful healing ministry travelled with Luke, the practising doctor (Colossians 4:14) and he even advised Timothy to take a little wine for his health's sake (1 Timothy 5:23). And Jesus said, "Those who are well have no need of a physician, but those who are sick." Matthew 9:12. And by saying this, we understand that He approved of the medical profession.

Health and long life are a result of following God's leading for us and others. As this is so important, why not re-read the chapter entitled 'Leading in health and healing'?

Relational Prosperity.

Our interactions with others keep improving as we

prosper spiritually and mentally. We prosper in our relationships partly because we were directed to change. Take this instruction as an example: "Do not let mercy and kindness and truth leave you [instead let these qualities define you]; Bind them [securely] around your neck, Write them on the tablet of your heart. So find favour and high esteem." Proverbs 3:3-4 Amplified Bible.

Here, we're directed to be gracious, tolerant, kind and honest with others. As a result, we have favour with them. We're led to change and empowered to change. Someone with a hot temper who harshly punishes anyone making a mistake reads this directive from God, they sense God convincing them that this text refers to their mean behaviour, they purpose to be merciful and kind and God gives them the ability to change.

Our change of behaviour pleases God and He blesses our relationships further. "And Jesus kept increasing in wisdom and stature, and in favour with God and people." Luke 2:52 New American Standard Bible.

As a result, our social and personal interactions grow more harmonious - family, friends, colleagues. In Proverbs 3:3-4 we're shown that high esteem and honour result from our good and honest behaviour. We gain a well-deserved reputation for integrity and balanced behaviour that smooths our way with others and opens opportunities.

Accomplishment Prosperity.

We want our loved ones to succeed and we take pride in them as they do, don't we? Well, that's how it is with God. He watches over you and bursts with joy when you succeed. He wants you to excel and He will lead you to achieve your best. We can fully trust that He has our interests at heart and so, everything He leads us in will help us from His unlimited perspective: "Trust in the Lord with all your heart, And lean not on your own understanding; In all your ways acknowledge Him, And He shall direct your paths." Proverbs 3:5-6.

As well as leading us to do well, God empowers us. Consider young David. He's not highly esteemed by his father and brothers and yet God knows his heart. He leads him from shepherd to king and leads him in all he does. Late in life, looking at all that was accomplished, he tells us it's because of God. This is what he declares to God before the people:

"Therefore David blessed the Lord before all the assembly; and David said: "Blessed are You, Lord God of Israel, our Father, forever and ever... In Your hand is power and might; In Your hand it is to make great And to give strength to all." 1 Chronicles 29:10, 12.

What things do you want to accomplish? Whatever they are, as you keep doing things the right way, pleasing God, He'll guide, help, empower, open doors and give you favour.

Professional Prosperity.

Whether it's a short-term position or a career you've been building over the years, expect God to be with you and lead you. Take Joseph, he's a young man with a good work ethic and competence and he's aware of God's leading. At seventeen, his father can entrust him to honestly appraise and report back on the work his brothers are doing with the livestock. Genesis 37:14. Sold into slavery, he gains professional recognition:

"The Lord was with Joseph, and he was a successful man... And his master (Potiphar) saw that the Lord was with him and that the Lord made all he did to prosper in his hand. So Joseph found favour in his sight, and served him. Then he made him overseer of his house, and all that he had he put under his authority. So it was, from the time that he had made him overseer of his house and all that he had, that the Lord blessed the Egyptian's house for Joseph's sake; and the blessing of the Lord was on all that he had in the house and in the field. Thus he left all that he had in Joseph's hand..." Genesis 39:2-6.

Falsely accused and thrown into prison he still prospers in his work: "the Lord was with Joseph and extended kindness to him, and gave him favour in the sight of the chief jailer. The chief jailer committed to Joseph's charge all the prisoners who were in the jail; so that whatever was done there, he was responsible for it. The chief jailer did not supervise anything under

Joseph's charge because the Lord was with him; and whatever he did, the Lord made to prosper." Genesis 39:21-23 NASB 1995.

Then, at thirty years of age he interprets Pharaoh's warning spirit dreams and provides a highly professional solution. His abilities are recognised and he goes from prison to Prime Minister. "Pharaoh said to Joseph, "Since God has informed you of all this, there is no one so discerning and wise as you are. You shall be over my house... See, I have set you over all the land of Egypt."" Genesis 39:39-41 NASB 1995.

The same leading and blessing applies to us: "Commit your works to the LORD [submit and trust them to Him], And your plans will succeed [if you respond to His will and guidance]." Proverbs 16:3 Amplified Bible.

Financial Prosperity.

When the bible refers to someone being wealthy or rich it often covers prosperity in all material ways. Today, for most of us, our material prosperity flows from money. We seldom barter: "I have herds of cattle; I'd like to purchase your land. Will you accept two hundred head of cattle for it?" Chances are, unless you really wanted cows, you'd be less than enthusiastic. And if you grew turnips? So, money is our preferred way of purchasing all we need and desire.

Abraham's servant said to Laban, "The Lord has greatly blessed my master, and he has become rich. He has given him sheep and cattle, silver and gold, menservants and maidservants, camels and donkeys." Genesis 24:35.

Tucked into that statement is silver and gold - currency, money. So, God greatly increased Abraham with money. God will lead us to gain money in honest, diligent ways so that what we offer in exchange to gain money is good value. That's so, whether it's goods, services or time as an employee or consultant. And so, God will be able to bless us financially and lead us to be debt free.

"The blessing of the LORD makes one rich, And He adds no sorrow with it." Proverbs 10:22. Godly financial gain ensures God's blessing to provide abundantly for our families, bless those around us, support God's work and worthy charities.

Material Prosperity.

The biblical understanding of wealth and riches refers to assets of all kinds that add to your life. So, when Abraham's most senior servant informed Laban that his master was rich, he had to cover in what ways...

"The LORD has greatly blessed my master, and he has become rich. (Here it comes...) He has given him sheep and cattle, silver and gold, menservants and maidservants, camels and donkeys." Genesis 24:35.

To Laban who had herds that was very successful. He understood that Abraham had an abundance of the material things that made his life good. And he understood that God was involved.

Abraham's material prosperity matched his lifestyle requirements. God will match yours and lead you and help you to prosper in the things you need. You probably wouldn't want camels; you'd rather your family travelled in cars. Donkeys? Think trucks. And it's unlikely that living in tents would be your thing. Now, a pleasant house with sufficient rooms and facilities? That's more in line with our needs today.

Expect that as you seek God in everything, and do things His way, He'll be involved, blessing you. "… it is He who gives you power to get wealth… " Deuteronomy 8:18.

After all, God gave you His word… "This is what the Lord says, your Redeemer, the Holy One of Israel: "I am the Lord your God, who teaches you how to succeed, who directs you in the path by which you should go." Isaiah 48:17 International Standard Version.

Prayer: "You love me and always have my best interests at heart. Lead me and help me to prosper in every way today and every day. Give me knowledge and wisdom and guide me in using all my skills to enrich my life and increase in *my prospering. Show me how I can use my blessings to bless others. Thank you for all you do for me."*

This is my time

God wants to lead you to bless you and prosper you abundantly for yourself and so that you can be blessing to others.

You explored the main categories:

- ✓ Spiritual Prosperity
- ✓ Mental Prosperity
- ✓ Physical Prosperity
- ✓ Relational Prosperity
- ✓ Accomplishment Prosperity
- ✓ Professional Prosperity
- ✓ Financial Prosperity
- ✓ Material Prosperity

-God will lead you, guide you and teach you in all of these and more. The following exercise will help you to maximise your receptivity to God prospering you.

-Take lots of paper and a pen. You're going to make rough notes.

-You're going to return to the expanded teaching on each of the categories which you read earlier.

-Re-read all of it but this time, you're going to watch for blocks. Yes, blocks. Let me give you an example:

-You're reading, 'Paul who had a powerful healing ministry travelled with Luke, the practising doctor (Colossians 4:14)...' You react positively and think "Thank you God for doctors and medical science!" Or, and this is what you're looking for, you feel irritated and feel that you must choose faith in healing and keep away from doctors and medicine. Okay, you've noted a block. Write it down and note the feelings and thoughts that go with it.

-In fact, how did you react just now? Did you feel good and have a positive response or did you feel yourself close up and think something hostile about that sentence and the medical services? Did you pick up any conflict in your thoughts and feelings?

-So, now, ask God to reveal any blocks, and then, take your time, to re-read those prosperity categories and record those blocks and the emotions and thoughts that went with each one.

-Afterward, return here to continue. We'll be dissolving those blocks.

How did you go?

Did you find blocks? That's normal and healthy. We all have to renew our thinking. And that's the key. You're now going to re-program your thoughts so that God can lead you to prosper in all ways.

Steps I will take

-Ask God if you missed anything to reveal what it is.

-Take each block and ask God to help you dissolve it in your thinking.

-Take a scripture to counter that block and to help you align your expectancy with what God says. Like this:

Block - having money makes you unspiritual.
Feelings - I want to increase financially but feel conflicted.

Solution - "The blessing of the LORD makes one rich, And He adds no sorrow with it." Proverbs 10:22 and "Both riches and honour come from You..." 1 Chronicles 29:12a and "The Lord has greatly blessed my master, and he has become rich. He has given him sheep and cattle, silver and gold, menservants and maidservants, camels and donkeys." Genesis 24:35.

-At the same time, ask God to reveal anything else you have to do to prosper in each way.

-Please take your time with this. It will be worth it because God wants to lead you to prosper in all, not just some things.

Coming up

The source of all this prospering in our lives is God. He's with us in a loving relationship in which He's teaching and guiding us. Led by God, our life can become a wonderful adventure...

GOD IS WITH YOU

"Where can I go from Your Spirit? Or flee from Your Presence? ...Your hand shall lead me, and You right hand shall hold me." Psalm 139:7 & 10.

Together, we've explored an abundance of ways that God leads you and how you can become more sensitive to that leading. And now, get ready for adventure!

When we wrote the title it could have just been 'He Leads Me Workbook' but no, that wasn't enough. You see, God has led us for a very, very long time and taught us so much about how it works. As a result, we've experienced amazing adventures through that leading - miracles, extraordinary provision, astonishing encounters, witnessed transformed lives and far more. We've lived everything we teach. It's real. It's true and it's an amazing adventure. And so, knowing all we know about God leading we had to add ... Adventures in God.

God wants to lead you into an exciting life packed with even more fulfilment.

My partner and I have shared with you some of our own real life adventures and the adventures that others experienced through the leading of God and the wonderful results that happened. And all because of God guiding, teaching being always with us.

God is always looking out for your best interests. Always with you… "Where can I go from Your Spirit? Or where can I flee from Your presence? …Your hand shall lead me, And Your right hand shall hold me." Psalm 139:7 & 10.

God is everywhere in our lives. His guiding Spirit is with us in every action and step we take. God is present in every moment and from His vantage point beyond time and space, He knows the full extent and scope of your life. He has amazing plans for you and will guide you all the way.

So, expect adventure, expect the extraordinary as you go on your very own adventure with God.

Prayer: "I thank You, my loving Creator for always being with me, always teaching and leading me. Help me now to take in the fullness of how You'll lead me into a life of greater fulfilment."

This is my time

It's been a pleasure exploring with you all the ways that God will lead you and how to be more sensitive to that leading. Without doubt, adventure lies ahead for you!

Before we say "Goodbye." ask yourself a few more questions...

-In each chapter you found steps you can take. Are there any that you need to keep working on?

-Do you need to learn more about something, for example, the gifts of the Spirit?

-God is always with you with your best interests at heart. Does that raise your confidence to follow His lead?

-Are you ready for God to lead you into an exciting life packed with even more fulfilment?

As you continue to work on anything you identified that needs your attention, you're ensuring that you'll get the most out of God leading you.

For us, it's immensely satisfying bringing you all our years of experience and knowledge as we shared in your journey of discovery. We're sure we'll travel together again, and so, "Goodbye for now, enjoy your exciting adventure and we'll meet again!"

HOW TO BLESS IN RETURN

The 'A Happy Walk Book' collection was created specifically to bring deep truths of our amazing God and reach as many people with sound, life changing truth as possible. To make them available and accessible to everyone we sell all these books at the lowest price possible. This is our way of sowing into your life and the lives of as many people as can be reached. Share with us in the joy of the harvest by spreading the news of this collection of books!

As you have been blessed by this book, take a moment to rate and review it here
https://www.amazon.co.uk/dp/B0B5VSRN5N

By doing this, you are improving the ranking of the book, which means it will be more visible on Amazon for Christians seeking meaningful and life changing books. You are helping fellow believers to find worthwhile books that will help them grow, prosper and enhance their lives. It's also an opportunity for you to testify the blessings that came from this book.

We also ask that you use your social media, church and family to help us promote the 'A Happy Walk Book' collection. As you've enjoyed the blessing in this book, please share the link so others may also receive the blessing.
https://www.amazon.co.uk/dp/B0B5VSRN5N

ABOUT THE AUTHORS

Learn more about Rennie Du Plessis at
https://www.amazon.com/author/rennieduplessis

Learn more about A Victor at
https://www.amazon.com/author/avictor

OTHER BOOKS BY THE AUTHORS

Follow us for all the latest releases and book offers.
Simply click follow authors here
https://www.amazon.com/author/rennieduplessis
https://www.amazon.com/author/avictor

Free Book 'Destiny Living Toolkit
https://www.subscribepage.com/faith-based-living

Tales out of Africa: Ordinary People having Extraordinary Encounters with God
https://www.amazon.co.uk/dp/B0957GZKMP

Destiny Living: A Practical Guide
https://www.amazon.co.uk/dp/1838021094

God's 'Thin Places' A Happy Walk Book
https://www.amazon.co.uk/dp/B09XLLCFVL

The Holy Spirit Book
https://www.amazon.com/gp/product/B086N4PRBT

Create your New Mind: Solve the Mind Puzzle and Create the Best Version of You
https://www.amazon.com/gp/product/B07Y5WC9GW

The Bridge of Possibility: Link the Physical and Spiritual to Release your Destiny
https://www.amazon.com/gp/product/B07Z787J3H

The Little Book on Church Counselling: Creating a Safe Place to bring Wholeness and Healing

https://www.amazon.com/gp/product/B07YGW8XNC

The Little Book on Church Counselling Leaders' Manual
https://www.amazon.co.uk/dp/1915349001

GIFTS for DESTINY and LIFE
https://www.amazon.co.uk/dp/1838021000

The Fruit of the Spirit: The way to whole and happy living
https://www.amazon.co.uk/dp/B08MYXVDQ6

Did I FORGET to tell YOU?
https://www.amazon.co.uk/dp/B09L4S3G6N

Make your Prayers work: A Happy Walk Book
https://www.amazon.co.uk/dp/B0B22YL7RX

GOALS: Christian Journal and Planner
https://www.amazon.co.uk/dp/1915349079

And more, including the new 'A Happy Walk Book' collection, check it out...
https://www.amazon.com/author/rennieduplessis

https://www.amazon.com/author/avictor

Printed in Great Britain
by Amazon